THE WEDDING PHOTOGRAPHER'S HANDBOOK

A QUICK AND DIRTY GUIDE TO TURNING YOUR SIDE HUSTLE INTO RELIABLE INCOME

J. ALLISON

"You can look at a picture for a week and never think of it again.
You can also look at a picture for a second and think of it all
your life."

– Joan Miro

DEDICATION

To John Bloyer Sr for teaching me you have to know the rules to break the rules, and that being a portrait photographer is a serious responsibility; one that puts you in charge of documenting someone's life in the most positive way. And if you're lucky, the clients will choose you to have this responsibility for the rest of their lives and possibly the lives of their future generations. John also taught me the guiding principles on the building blocks needed to gain the respect of an entire local community.

To Charlie Trotter for teaching me no job is too cheap. Every budget needs a photographer, so make a package that can fit every budget.

To Bill Greensmith for teaching me the exquisite art of cultural intelligence, the delicacy of working therein, and to be passionate about something, even if it's not photography.

To Ed Faller for teaching me that to be a successful wedding photographer, you have to have an arsenal of poses while simultaneously being a comedian. He also taught me the psychology of dealing with Bridezillas and their mothers.

To Rick Niblett and Donna Pulliam for teaching me the most efficient way to photograph a wedding from beginning to end that covers every single base in the shortest amount of time. They taught me how to work smarter, not harder and still get a guaranteed sit down meal with the guests at the reception.

PREFACE

Wedding Photography can be a great business. It's generally a happy environment and there's never a shortage of people getting married. As a source of income for you the photographer, it is reliable and you get paid up front.

However, it's not all roses. It is hard work...I mean, really physically, emotionally, and mentally demanding. There are many professional photographers out there that eventually 'hang up their gloves' per se, due to the demanding nature of this business. I am not ashamed to admit that I am one of those photographers.

I spent a better part of twelve years doing weddings as a full-time job. I worked for three different professional studios before going out on my own. Ultimately, I chose to take a different career path and now use my photography skills in a different way. But as I reflect on my career path as a whole, I keep thinking to myself that there's so much school doesn't teach you about the business of working in the arts. Why should all of this insider knowledge die with me switching careers? I decided, it shouldn't, and this is why I'm writing this book.

A few years ago, I ran small Meetup workshops in St. Louis where I taught and shared everything I know about the business of wedding photography. We were 88 members strong and it was a solid group. I loved being able to help photographers make the transition from other types of photography to wedding photography. Then in a turn of events, my new career path pulled me back to New York City. I quickly contacted all of my old colleagues in the professional photography industry and tried to find a replacement instructor. Time ran out before I could find anyone willing to take on the challenge. Turns out most photographers are more happy working than teaching. And I'll admit there's much more money in working than teaching, so that probably added to my failure in finding a replacement. Since then, all of the materials I had created for instruction remained dormant. That is, until now.

This book won't teach you everything you need to know about this business, but it will most certainly give you a huge advantage compared to someone else going at it alone. To put it another way, I worked at three different professional studios, all with mentors carrying 20+ years of experience doing it in their own way. So 20+20+20+ my 10 years = 70 combined years of knowledge through experience. This book will teach you what works, what doesn't, and why - all in a short, yet comprehensive guide.

1. FINDING CLIENTS

When you are just starting out, you might consider doing weddings pro-bono with a model release trade-off just to get the experience and start building your portfolio of work. Have your clients sign that model release so you can legally use the images for your portfolio and future advertising. This is important. Do it before the wedding, not after. If you don't have this signed document, and you use someone's image or likeness without his or her written consent, you're asking for trouble.

I usually advise against using family members as clients because there's too much at stake if something goes wrong. However, I understand you have to start somewhere, so if this is the case, then you should at the very least get a signed model release, but still go through the contract. (You can tell them you need the practice if they question why you're being so formal), and at the very end where you input the dollar amount, put the amount you would normally charge. Then under payments you can change the section to say 'professional discount.' Then put that same number you would normally charge so that the final amount due totals out to $0. This may just sound like extra work, but it's good for two reasons.

1. It gives you practice walking through some of this stuff with the clients and helps you become more comfortable in a professional role.

2. This puts a price on what you are worth, but still shows your client you are generous in offering it for $0. In other words, it gives your future clients (family or not) a perceived value of what you are offering - that your time and experience as a professional is worth something. People will place a higher value on something with a price, as opposed to something that started at $0.

You might also consider contacting a professional studio and asking if you can work as an intern/wedding assistant so that you can get some hands on experience without the pressure of everything being solely on your shoulders. Keep in mind, not all studios operate the same way so don't be surprised if you see a major difference in how they run the show. The idea is to work enough to get some real experience, so when you *do* go out on your own, you will be ready.

Once you've got a few weddings under your belt, consider making your website. You'll want a one-page landing page at the very least that says who you are, what you do, a few examples, and how to contact you. Don't worry if you don't know how out build a website. There are great DIY services out there made for people who don't know how to code like Square Space, free Google sites, and my favorite, www.Wix.com. You can make a super impressive website in one weekend.

. . .

Once you have all this done, it's time to expand your reach for clients. Most, if not all my clients are word of mouth referrals. Those are the best because:

- It's free
- It builds your reputation in the local community as a professional
- Your client base grows on its own as long as you keep doing good work and keep your clients happy.
- You might already have a heads up on what it's like to work with the clients based on past work you've done with them or their relatives.

After direct referrals, consider renting a booth at local bridal fairs or hosting free virtual bridal events. Bridal fairs can cost anywhere from a few hundred to several thousand to get a booth, but it's great for new client leads. You might even consider running a raffle that gives away a canvas print or bridal session, or something similar. At the minimum this can help you acquire email leads and the winner might end up booking you for the actual wedding day...even if not, it's a way to make contact for possible future work. *A side note on email campaigns. Try using a service like Mail Chimp, or Constant Contact. It makes sending professional looking email campaigns a breeze and offers step-by-step guidance. You can also add a widget to you website; which streamlines the process.

Speaking of future work, follow up with your clients a few months after the event. Ask them if they have any feedback for you and/or if they would be willing to complete a short survey or write a testimonial that you can use for your website. You can use Google Forms or a site called Typeform. You might even offer a free holiday portrait session for their time.

Get involved with your local Chamber of Commerce, or consider donating free mini sessions at charity events. You might be thinking yeah, but that's not going to guarantee work for me, and you're right. You might take a hit once in a while, but it does put your name out there and it gives you a chance to distribute business cards and meet possible future clients.

If there's one thing I hope you are starting to notice it's that the actual 'taking pictures part' is only a small piece of what it takes to be successful.. and this goes for any business.

2. THE CONSULTATION

You might be saying, 'but I don't even know how to talk to clients, let alone plan all this out.' Have no fear, below is a step-by-step guide on what to say at your first client meeting. This is assuming you've already made at least the initial verbal agreement that you are available for the day of their wedding.

One very important thing to remember about differentiating yourself from other photographers is that as a professional, you do this all the time. *Clients DON'T* get married every weekend, but *you DO* photograph weddings every weekend, or at least you will be soon. This means you have an advantage! Meaning, you know how the day will play out, what's expected, the norms, or what will fail every time no matter how bad the client thinks it 'will just work out'.

The point is if you can plan accordingly to get everything done beforehand, this is the best and most efficient scenario for everyone involved. The reception is for celebrating, not picture studio time. You should be able to use this knowledge of experience to your advantage. Knowing things like this and being able to avoid catastrophe by planning ahead helps your clients to know they are in good hands.

Another thing to remember; you are interviewing them just as much as they are interviewing you. One of the worst possible things is to get stuck with a bad client. There are always exceptions to the rule, but in general you will want to avoid clients that:

1. Wait until the very last minute to find a photographer. This shows that of all the wedding vendors, photography is not high on their list of priorities and therefore not as important. This also usually means they don't understand the value a professional photographer brings and will most likely be expecting a rock bottom price. On average my clients should expect 15-20% of their wedding budget to go toward photography. You have to remember that you don't get to work less because they want to spend less. You will have to work just as hard if not harder for the clients looking for bargain photographers, so you're best option is to refer them to 'student photographers'. That being said, everyone has to start somewhere. Get a few good weddings under your belt, gain some experience, then by word of mouth you'll have enough clients to be choosy.

2. Give you a bad gut feeling. If they found you through an email or unknown source, watch out for scammers. I once had a scammer that found me on the web and turned out to be a wire transfer scam. He had an elaborate story – all through email - about needing to book a photographer right away, that he and his future bride were moving to Germany and that they just wanted to book me

immediately to secure the date but he could never meet in person. After more probing and detective work with authorities, we determined it was indeed a scam. Follow your gut in these situations and never get into something for which you are not 100% comfortable.

3. Refuse to pay you upfront. The rate of quick divorce and willingness to jump into debt is unfortunate in this country, but nearly all wedding industry vendors require upfront payment. This is standard so if your client refuses, or tries to work out payment plans for after the wedding, walk away. Trust me, it's not worth it. Typically, you need to charge a retainer fee (nonrefundable) to hold the date then split into one or two more payments and last payment is due two weeks before the wedding. Again, this is the norm with any wedding vendor, so it shouldn't be a surprise to your client either if they've already booked other vendors.

4. Bridezillas, Divas, or clients who are already signed with your 'less-preferred' vendors. An example would be a local wedding venue that has a horrible reputation for working with any other wedding vendor. Two specific examples: 'Venue A' has a 'wedding coordinator who wants to run the show and is notorious for being verbally abusive and running photographers around like they are cattle." Or "We are having our secondary location at the most popular place in ___" aka the same place everyone and their mom wants pictures on Saturday afternoon. Traffic and parking will be worse than rush hour and you will have to fight other photographers for 5 minutes by the 'special fountain'. Then when you finally get your chance, you have other wedding party bystanders in the background of your pictures. There are **plenty** of other places to create gorgeous photographs; private or lesser

known locations work best. See if the clients are willing to try another location.

So here's a sample script with some anecdotal snippets in between the dialogue. With a smile start out by saying...

"Hi ____ and ____, It is so nice to meet you! How did you hear about me?" (This is important. If it's a direct referral then usually you are in the clear.)

"That's great. Yeah I remember their wedding. It was a lot of fun and it's always nice to work with great people like __ & ____.

Before we get started I just want to make sure we are all on the same page. We know you have a choice in photographers, and we photographers also have a set of standards that we like to abide by as professionals, so we like to interview our potential clients just to make sure we are a good match before making any agreements or signing any contracts. Is that OK with you?"

"Um Sure?"

"OK great! Yeah it's very rare that we don't end up being a good match. I just like to throw it out there so there are no surprises.

So tell me about your day! I'm excited to hear what you have planned so far, what kind of ideas do you have for the photography? What other vendors are you meeting with and/or contracts you have signed?"

Let them talk about their plans and actively listen. You can learn a ton about people, and possibly what it will be like to work with them over the next few months just by listening to how they talk about things. If you hear things like "Yeah we don't really even like pictures, but our parents want us to do it. Honestly we could care less. We think wedding pictures are contrived and cheesy.". Or on the opposite end, " I have everything planned out just like I want, down to the minute and I always get my way!" –You may have a harder time working with these clients as opposed to clients that are enthusiastic about photography, or willing to be flexible with their itinerary. I'm not saying it is not a good match, just be aware of how these kinds of clients might play out when the stakes are high and the stresses of the wedding day approach, and what they will be like to deal with after the wedding with post production.

Now back to the consultation.

If they mention they want pictures at the 'most popular fountain in the city' ask if they are willing to try another location and explain the reasoning mentioned earlier. If they won't budge, it might be a good time to say,

> "Well, I have to say I think you two are great, and you're a lovely couple, and there's no doubt you are going to have a gorgeous wedding, but unfortunately I think you might be better suited for

another photographer. I may be able to refer you to someone if you like?"

The same goes if they mention they've already booked with a 'less-preferred vendor'. It might be in your interest to politely decline.

After they've talked through their needs and you've assessed the relationship might be a good fit, continue by saying,

"Wow it sounds like you've done your homework! All of this sounds really exciting. I love your enthusiasm for bringing this all together. You two are going to have an awesome wedding!

Now if I may, I'd like to spend a little time talking about our typical work-flow as photographers. Since we do this every weekend, we've managed to perfect the itinerary of the day, to cover all the pictures people usually request, AND maximize the amount of time you get with your family and guests.. because let's face it, nobody likes a photographer that hogs the wedding couple all day like it's his private photo shoot. This is YOUR day to celebrate YOU. It's not OUR day, and we respect that.

We've also been doing this a long time and need to be in sync with many of the other wedding vendors that day. This means we have established relationships with them because we work with them often. Generally, the photographer keeps everyone on schedule during the day, and the DJ takes over and keeps everyone on schedule at the reception. We are known to work behind the scenes with the florist, the officiant, wedding coordinators, the limo driver, the caterer, and the DJ to make your day run smooth as silk. THIS is what differentiates us from 'student or amateur photographers'. There are things that go on behind the scenes that you are never made aware of, and rightly so. You shouldn't have to worry about those things. That's our job. We've got this down to a science.

So, that being said, here's how we like to do things. If we choose to proceed, after we sign the contract, I'll have you fill out an information sheet with the vital details, such as: locations with addresses and phone numbers, members of the wedding party, etc. If needed, I will contact your other wedding vendors to discuss the details of your event and/or any of their requirements as well. An example: Some churches strictly prohibit flash photography during the ceremony, and only allow 30 minutes for all of the family portraits up at the altar. I've even had churches turn out the lights and close the doors. They book weddings back to back on some days. This is typical and completely normal, but don't worry our itinerary takes this in to account. Another example: Some transportation providers only have a limited amounted of time with you, the client, before they need to go to their next event, but YOU want pictures with the limo at the reception so I arrange this so they can still leave on time, and you get your limo pictures."

Back to The Big Day...

We start one hour before the wedding, no more, no less. Usually the flowers aren't there before this and we need them before we can do any pictures anyway. Inevitably someone WILL be late so it's your job to tell everyone we are starting 1.5-2 hours beforehand. This is at your discretion. If your wedding party is a fairly responsible bunch, usually just adding a half hour before the time is fine. So if your wedding is at 2 p.m., tell everyone we are starting pictures at 12:30 p.m.

We will start with the girls. We need the bride, the bridesmaids, flower girl, and the bride's parents. We will do the bride by herself, the bride with each bridesmaid, the mother with the bride, the father with the bride, mother and father together, and bride with any siblings that are bridesmaids. We will also do photo-journalistic style photographs of the bride getting ready.

From here we move on to the guys. They usually show up later so this works out perfect. This is a half hour before the ceremony somewhere away from the bridal party. The same people are needed for the same series of photographs: the groom, his groomsmen, including ring bearer and ushers, and his parents. We also take photo-journalistic style of the guys getting ready, pinning boutonnières, etc.

When it's time, we will follow the bride and the bridal party up to the aisle. We take pictures of the father with the bride and then head to the center of the aisle. We try to remain hidden during the ceremony. The focus should be on YOU not US. A good photographer can take pictures. A great photographer can take pictures and remain hidden like a ninja. We get the grandparents walking down the aisle, the bridesmaids, the bride, etc. Then the hand off, then retreat to the back of the church and use lenses to get close ups if we need to. If possible we will place a secondary camera in the balcony or another location. Our goal is to get gorgeous images, yet remain as unnoticeable as possible. After the ceremony, we get the kiss, you two coming back up the aisle, and the couples walking back up the aisle.

At this time, you might be thinking of a receiving line, but depending on your venue and how much time we have to get pictures afterwards, we strongly advise against this. We also advise against the bride and groom releasing the pews, and instead suggest receiving your guests at the reception after dinner. The reasoning is that receiving lines typically take at least 30-45 minutes. If your venue only allows 30 minutes for all of your family photographs, then you've just traded all your 'picture taking time' for 'receiving line time'. Also people are happier after they've eaten. You can have your maid of honor or best man make an announcement to any guests waiting for you in the lobby. If you want to do a bubbles picture leaving the ceremony, this can be staged as people are filing out the church. Then they can be free to go and no one is left standing around waiting...which your guests will appreciate.

Before the big day, you should advise your extended family and wedding party that you want to take pictures with, (aunts uncles, grandparents, etc.) that they will be needed **immediately after the ceremony up at the altar.** Tell them not to leave for any reason. This means no quick trips to the convenient store, no taking things out to the car, etc. Remember we only have a half hour to do EVERY family picture. The sooner everyone cooperates the faster we can get the pictures done, so you can be on your way.

We start with the two of you and your grandparents first, so they can relax and leave first. We will then photograph your immediate families on brides side, or grooms side, whomever is ready to go. Then we'll add extended family for that side.

Switch sides (bride's family or groom's family) and repeat – The two of you plus groom's immediate family, then add extended family. If you start to see a pattern here, it's not by accident it's by design. By strategically adding members to the group formation depending on relation, we can maximize the time for pictures and minimize physically moving people around unnecessarily.

Then, we do a last call for any other family members you requested that we didn't get. Now the extended family is free to go.

Now the wedding party. We'll start with the girls. All the bridesmaids, flower girl, and the two of you. We then take away the bride for the groom and bridesmaid shot, then add the bride and groomsmen. (We could start with the guys, but usually guys are easier to move around than girls in dresses and heels, so this is why we add them instead of moving the girls around.) Then we take away the bridesmaids for the bride with groomsmen picture, etc. Then a few pictures of just the two of you.

If all of this is overwhelming, don't worry, just remember: grandparents, then extended family, then wedding party, then you.

From here we move on to the second location and do more pictures with the wedding party and the two of you. Typically the ushers, flower girl, and ring bearer skip this part, but that's up to you. The second location takes usually about 30-45 minutes, and depends on when your reception starts.

At the reception, we get all of the traditional events, the walking in processional, the dances, the cake, the garter and bouquet toss, etc. We'll do a few artsy pictures of memorabilia, flowers, party décor, etc. We usually leave a little while after the main reception events. We used to stay until the very end and photograph everything, but found that the later it gets, the more 'interesting' the pictures, especially if there's alcohol involved, and the pictures are, to put it gently, 'unbecoming' of you and your guests. Plus, at that point it's been a full work day for us too, usually at least 8 - 10 hours straight, ... and in that time, we've managed to cover every major event including extra requests, so logically there's no point in us just hanging around to get 'drunk blackmail pictures of your guests'. We will of course check with you to make sure we didn't miss anything before making our departure.

Lastly, this brings me to an important part of our working agreement. Since we commit to working a full day, in most cases this means at least an eight-hour day, but in some cases more, we go into this knowing that we will not get regular breaks, and we cannot clock out for lunch or dinner. We do however, still need time to eat. Since this will be contingent on the wedding day schedule, this means we will require a meal seated with the guests. We also need to be seated with the guests so that we can be ready to go at a moment's notice if something spontaneous happens that needs to be photographed. For this reason, we must respectfully decline any offers for sack lunches in the back of the kitchen. If providing us a meal with the guests is going to be a problem, we need to know well in advance so that we can adjust the contract to provide us ample time to go elsewhere for a food break.

We also must kindly decline any alcohol if offered. We understand some couples want us to celebrate with them after we are finished working, but we believe this diminishes our reputation as professionals.

And that's it! I'm not sure if you've interviewed with other photographers or are just starting your search, but we welcome you to check out other photographers. In fact, we encourage it. Ask lots of questions, and if you feel we are the right fit for your needs, we'd love to have you as clients!"

By this point your future clients should be feeling pretty comfortable that they've chosen the right photographer, but encourage them to keep exploring. If you want to sweeten the pot a little to close the deal in a timely manner, you could offer a limited time bonus of some sort for booking within the next three days. But don't be pushy! This is a big decision for them, and you should have enough confidence that your work and professionalism will help them to choose you.

3. THE CONTRACT

Your client is ready to book you. Great! Here's what you need to make it official. Hopefully you already have insurance for your business. If not, check out the photographer's links in the appendix. (The PPA offers indemnification insurance for photographers and also has plans that will cover your equipment.) So let's say you have all that and are ready to sign the paper work. I've given you samples; which you can copy and paste into your own letterhead and change things to fit your needs. There are also links within the appropriate section where you can download directly to edit.

Go through the terms and conditions with your clients. Make sure they understand everything and ask questions if they don't. Most of the things are precautionary and up to your discretion whether or not you want to enforce them. You can tell your clients this too.

My disclaimer, " I am not an attorney and do not provide legal advice. This contract is a sample only and you should take precautions of your own to tailor it to your specific needs, which may include hiring your own attorney." I've added notation in orange as explanatory notes for you. Take those parts out in the final draft.

4. WEDDING PHOTOGRAPHY CONTRACT

I've added the fields below I would typically include in a contract, along with commentary about certain sections. For convenience, you can also download and edit your own at: https://drive.google.com/file/d/ 1tXVsIzeXQvAquumWmGovHSGeHWX5Ms9c/view?usp=sharing

Clients:

Event Date:

Order Number (office use):

Bride's Name:

Phone:

Email:

Address

:

:

:

Groom's Name:

Phone:

Email:

Address

:

:

:

Couple's future address (if different than above)

:

:

:

Locations for Photography

[ ] Ceremony Location:

Address

:

:

Time:

Phone:

[ ] Secondary Location:

Address

:

:

Time:

Phone:

[ ] Reception Location:

Address

:

:

Time:

Phone:

Special Services Required

:

:

Charges

The package fee is based on the Photographer's Standard Price List and includes the photographs described therein. If the fee is not based on a package but is a session fee, all photographs shall be billed in addition to the fee and in accordance with the Standard Price List. In addition to either the package fee or the session fee, the extra charges set forth below shall be billed if and when incurred.

[ ] Package Fee (Package number) $__________

[ ] Fee Without Package $__________

[ ] Overtime $__________

[ ] Travel $__________

Subtotal $__________

Sales tax $__________

Total Due $__________ Less retainer fee $__________

Balance Due by:______ $__________

Agreement applies to Terms and Conditions Below

Travel is included for up to 1 hour drive time from the ceremony. Any mileage beyond that I usually charge an additional fee. For example the wedding is in town, but the reception is at a winery three hours away. This can quickly turn into a 15 hour day so you may want to charge a mileage fee for those extra two hours.)

Overtime. *Your full-day package should be a full*

working day. That means eight hours, not 16. This is to discourage the bride who says, "I want you to start by taking pictures of me at 7 am at the hair salon!" Her girlfriends can get this with cell phones, but if these pictures are really so important that it will turn into a 16-hour workday for you, you should be compensated.)

Terms and Conditions

1. Exclusive Photographer. The Photographer shall be the exclusive photographer retained by the Client for the purpose of photographing the wedding. Family and friends of the Client shall be permitted to photograph the wedding as long as they shall not interfere with the Photographer's duties.

This is really just to weed out Aunt Nancy standing in front of your camera the whole time while you're up at the alter after the ceremony hustling to get all your pictures done in a half hour. I tell this to the client and say what I usually do is, make an announcement at the beginning of pictures. I say "Attention please, I want to thank everyone for being on time and ready to go. I know you are all hungry and anxious to get to the reception so the quicker we can get through this, the faster we can head over to the celebration. The only thing I ask is that you let me get my pictures first because they paid me to be here, then I'll give you a moment to get yours. Sound good?"

2. Retainer Fee and Payment. The Client shall make a retainer fee payment to retain the Photographer to perform the services specified herein. At such time as this order is completed, the retainer fee shall be applied to reduce the total cost and Client shall pay the balance due. Total balance will be paid one week prior to event. Failure to finalize payment prior to event will null and void this contract. The retainer fee is not refundable under any circumstances.

> *(**Retainer fee.** You should never charge 'deposits' because deposits can legally be required to be refunded. You place a deposit on physical goods, not services. Charge a retainer fee because that's what it is. They are paying you to hold and retain that specific date for them. You are going to turn away other work in return so if they cancel, you will lose out on the rest of the money. You will most likely not be able to re-book another wedding in such a short amount of time so at the very least you should make it clear that this is a non-refundable retainer fee. You can always offer a studio credit if they cancel; which they can use for other portraits at a future date.)*

3. Cancellation. If the Client shall cancel this Agreement thirty (30) or more calendar days before the wedding date, any further payments beyond the retainer fee to the Photographer shall be refunded in full. If Client shall cancel within thirty days of the wedding date and if the Photographer does not obtain another assignment for that date, liquidated damages shall be charged in a reasonable amount not to exceed the contracted amount.

4.Photographic Materials. All photographic materials, including but not limited to digital files, proofs, previews, etc. shall be the exclusive property of the Photographer unless transfer of copyright ownership has been arranged. In the case of transfer of ownership, the client will obtain a copyright release form the photographer. The Photographer shall either make a digital compilation of the images, OR a website with previews available to the Client for the purpose of selecting photographs for print ordering.

5. Copyright and Reproductions. The Photographer shall own the copyright in all images created and shall have the exclusive right to make reproductions unless otherwise arranged. The Photographer shall only make reproductions for the Client or for the Photographer's portfolio, samples, self-promotions, entry in photographic contests or art exhibitions, editorial use, or for display within or on the outside of the Photographer's studio. If the Photographer desires to make other uses, the Photographer shall not do so without first obtaining the written permission of the Client.

6. Client's Usage. The Client is obtaining prints for personal use only, and shall not sell said prints or authorize any reproductions thereof by parties other than the Photographer unless Client obtains the copyright release. If Client is obtaining a print or digital file for newspaper announcement of the wedding, Photographer authorizes Client to reproduce the print in this manner. In such event, Client shall request that the newspaper run a credit for the Photographer adjacent to the photograph, but shall have no liability if the newspaper refuses or omits to do so.

7. Failure to Perform. If the Photographer cannot perform this Agreement due to a fire or other casualty, strike, act of God, or other cause beyond the control of the parties, or due to Photographer's illness, then the Photographer shall return the payments beyond the retainer fee to the Client but shall have no further liability with respect to the Agreement. This limitation on liability shall also apply in the event that photographic materials are damaged in processing, lost through camera malfunction, lost in the mail, or otherwise lost or damaged without fault on the part of the Photographer. In the event the Photographer fails to perform for any other reason, the Photographer shall not be liable for any amount in excess of the retail value of the Client's order.

8. Photographer. The Photographer may substitute another photographer to take the photographs in the event of Photographer's illness or of scheduling conflicts. In the event of such substitution, Photographer warrants that the photographer taking the photographs shall be a competent professional.

9.Inherent Qualities. Client is aware that color dyes in photographic prints may fade or discolor over time due to the inherent qualities of dyes, and Client releases Photographer from any liability for any claims whatsoever based upon fading or discoloration due to such inherent qualities.

. . .

10. Photographer's Standard Price List. The charges in this Agreement are based on the Photographer's Standard Price List. This price list is adjusted periodically and future orders shall be charged at the prices in effect at the time when the order is placed.

11. Client's Originals. If the Client is providing original prints, negatives, or transparencies owned by the Client to the Photographer for duplication, framing, reference, or any other purpose, in the event of loss or damage the Photographer shall not be liable for an amount in excess of $(insert dollar amount) per image.

12. Arbitration. All disputes arising under this Agreement shall be submitted to binding arbitration before (insert date) in the following location (insert location) and the arbitration award may be entered for judgment in any court having jurisdiction thereof. Notwithstanding the foregoing, either party may refuse to arbitrate when the dispute is for a sum less than $(insert dollar amount).

13. Miscellany. This Agreement incorporates the entire understanding of the parties. Any modifications of this Agreement must be in writing and signed by both parties. Any waiver of a breach or default hereunder shall not be deemed a waiver of a subsequent breach or default of either the same provision or any other provision of this Agreement. This Agreement shall be governed by the laws of the State of (insert state).

The parties have read this Agreement, agree to all its terms, and acknowledge receipt of a complete copy of the Agreement signed by both parties. Each person signing as Client below shall be fully responsible for ensuring that full payment is made pursuant to the terms of this Agreement.

Client (sign):

Client (print):

Date:

Client (sign):

Client (print):

Date:

Photographer (sign) :

Photographer (print):

Date:

5. THE PICTURE LIST

You booked the wedding, you have all the paperwork, the client has paid their retainer fee, and you feel good about how things are coming together. Then all of a sudden you get this crazy 'must-have shots' list the bride found in a magazine even though you've already went through the detailed plan for the day which maximized the time with the guests, and covered all the bases already. Don't fret. This is normal. You have to understand the clients are excited about this day and are just trying to communicate what they want. It's not their fault. They don't know that it's probably magazine editors that write these lists, not real photographers that do this for a living.

I've included an example of a very popular magazine's suggested 'must-have' list with critical notation of why some of these requests are not practical, how they end up creating way more work than necessary, and how some of these suggestions could actually disrupt the delicate balance needed between you and other wedding vendors.. **After this list I will provide the 'Real**

Must-Have list' so that your assistant can keep it on the clipboard and check off as you go.

"Real-Simple" Magazine's Must-Take Wedding Photo Checklist

The author: "A week or so before the ceremony, supply the photographer with a list of moments that are important to you. Pick and choose from these 79 photo ops, keeping in mind that each shot should take about four minutes."

(Well, it's nice he /she assumes we would have the luxury of four minutes to take each picture. In reality this list averages to more like an image every 30 seconds.)

Getting Ready

(Most of these you are going to get anyway through your photo-journalistic style stuff while you are waiting for them to get ready for the formal portraits.)

- *Bride with her bridesmaids*
- *Bride having her hair styled and makeup applied*
- *Bride's gown hanging on a padded hanger, spread on the bed, or draped over a chair*
- *Still life shots of the bride's shoes, jewelry, something old, something new, something borrowed, and something blue*
- *Detailed shots of the bride's and bridesmaids' bouquets*
- *Candid shots of the bridesmaids getting dressed*
- *Mother buttoning or zipping up the bride's dress*
- *Mother helping the bride with one last detail, such as the veil*

- *Full-length shot of the bride in her gown, looking at herself in a mirror*
- *Bridesmaids reacting to the bride in her gown*
- *Father seeing the bride in her gown*
- *Bride with her parents and siblings* (Just do the parents, not the siblings at this point. Do the siblings afterwards at the alter with the family portraits. Example: It doesn't make sense to expect a brother who's oftentimes a groomsmen, to be both here with his sister (the bride), AND getting ready with the guys at the same time. It's too much running around, and you're going to photograph the family up at the alter afterwards anyway.)

- *Bride with her bridesmaids*
- *Groom getting ready with his father and groomsmen*
- *Close-up shot of the wedding bands*
- *Groom with his parents and siblings* (Same thing as above. Photograph the parents, but leave the siblings for after the ceremony.)
- *Groom with the best man*
- *Groom with his groomsmen*
- *Groomsmen putting on boutonnières or ties*
- *Bride and groom separately making their way to the ceremony* (OK this one is not even logical. The venue usually places the bridal party far away from the groomsmen before the ceremony so the groom won't accidentally see the bride beforehand. There's no way you can be at two different places at the same time. Just get the bride.)
- *Exterior and interior shots of the site before guests arrive*
- *Groom walking down the aisle with his mother*
- *Close-up of groom's expression while waiting for the bride* (Just get him when he SEES the bride. If you get him while he's

waiting it will be a deer-in-headlights-look and it's terribly unflattering.)

- *Bridal party walking down the aisle*
- *Both sets of grandparents walking down the aisle*
- *Bride and her escort waiting to walk down the aisle*
- *Close-up of bride just before she makes her entrance*
- *Bride and her escort walking down the aisle*
- *Groom reacting to bride walking down the aisle*
- *Bride's escort giving her away*
- *Bride and groom at the altar or the chuppah*
- ~~*Both sets of parents watching the ceremony*~~ (Nope. You're not supposed to be up there anyway.)
- *Wide shot of the altar or chuppah, from the guests' point of view*
- ~~*Wide shot of the guests, from the couple's point of view*~~ (Again, you are not supposed to be up there in the front! Taking this shot makes you "the obnoxious photographer", and could get you blacklisted from the venue.)
- *Special moments, such as the candle lighting and the readings*
- *Close-up of the bride and groom as they recite their vows* (don't worry about close ups unless you have a telephoto lens. You can always crop close if they really want it.)
- *Close-up of the bride and groom's hands as they exchange rings*
- *The kiss!* (Don't miss this one, but watch out! Sometimes they do it without a big announcement, so as they walk towards you to exit the church, have them pause and kiss again. This way you have 'a kiss' shot for sure!)
- *Close-up of the newlyweds immediately after the ceremony*
- ~~*Bride and groom hugging family and friends*~~ (No, No, No, No. We've already talked about why it's a disaster to do receiving lines.)
- *Bride showing off her wedding ring to her bridesmaids*
- *Bride and groom leaving the ceremony site*

- ***Before the Reception (or Ceremony)***
- *Bride and groom together*
- *Bride with her mother* (Do this before the wedding)
- *Bride with her father* (Do this before the wedding)
- *Bride with both parents* (Do this before the wedding)
- *Bride with her entire immediate family*
- *Groom with his mother* (Do this before the wedding)
- *Groom with his father* (Do this before the wedding)
- *Groom with both parents* (Do this before the wedding)
- *Groom with his entire immediate family*
- *Bride and groom with bride's family*
- *Bride and groom with groom's family*
- *Bride and groom with both sets of parents*
- *Bride and groom with immediate family members from both sides*
- *Bride and groom with bridesmaids*
- *Bride and groom with groomsmen*
- *Bride and groom with flower girl and ring bearer*
- *Bride and groom with entire wedding party*
- *Exterior and interior shots of the site before the guests arrive*
- *Still-life shots of place cards, menus, centerpieces, decorations, table settings, favors, and Champagne glasses* (Do this towards the end of the night when there's no one sitting at the head table.)
- *The cake*
- *Hors d'oeuvre and specialty drinks*
- *Guests arriving and signing the guest book*
- *Bride and groom arriving*
- *Close-ups of friends and family making toasts* (Maid of Honor, Best Man, Bride & Groom, or whoever else speaks – that's all. These are more important – and you'll pose an additional fake one with the bride and groom right after the toast.)

- *Bride and groom sipping Champagne at their table*
- *Bride and groom speaking with guests*
- *Bride and groom's first dance*
- *Bride dancing with her father*
- *Groom dancing with his mother*
- *Parents and grandparents dancing*
- *Wedding party dancing*
- *Musicians, DJ, and/or entertainers performing*
- *Guests dancing*
- *Bride and groom dancing with the bridal party*
- *Bride and groom cutting the cake*
- *Bouquet toss*
- ~~*Newlyweds' vehicle*~~ Bride and groom leaving the reception (I usually don't stay for this unless it is specifically requested.)

6. THE REAL MUST-HAVE SHOT LIST

Most of these will be posed and the candid shots should be self-explanatory. But the idea is that weddings happen so fast and there are no redoes so it's a good idea to get a quick posed one before the real one even if it seems to fit into the candid category. An example is the garter and bouquet toss. Sometimes the groom doesn't wait for the count of three from the DJ, and will just fling the garter to his buddies with no warning. If you can jump in right after he takes it off her leg and say, "hey can I get a quick shot of you holding the garter. Cheese!" – and click. Then you can get the real one as it happens, but have the posed one as a backup. Also the real action shots are not as flattering for faces, expressions, etc. so having a quick posed version in addition is the safest bet.

To make things easier for you, this shot list is fairly close to the chronological order of the day. The checklist is the must-have list, but you should also be taking photo-journalistic style pictures in addition to, and in between, pictures on this lists. I've made a copy you can download, make your own, and print out at: https://drive.

google.com/file/d/18cg4gIBtpnWa5CZ3nWB-QljeCh74nfxF/view?
usp=sharing

Pre Ceremony

1. Outside wide-angle of church or venue

2. Close-up of the sign for church or venue

(Don't forget they need the flowers for all these, including boutonnières.)

3. Bride Alone

4. Bride with Maid of Honor

5. Bride with each bridesmaid individually

6. Bride with flower Girl

7. Bride with program or guest book attendants

8. Detail shots: back of dress, flowers, shoes, jewelry, etc.

9. Bride with Mom

10. Bride with Dad

11. Bride with both parents

12. Bride with other parents

____

13. Groom alone

14. Groom with Best Man

15. Groom with Groomsmen individually

16. Groom with Ring Bearer

17. Close up of Rings (Usually the best man has them)

18. Detail shots: Cuff links, ties, boutonnières

19. Groom with Mom

20. Groom with Dad

21. Groom with both parents

22. Groom with other parents

———————

23. Program or Guest Book Attendants

24. Detail shots: Program, Guest Book, Bubble basket, etc.

Ceremony

25. Bride and Dad from back of church

26. Ushers

27. Grandparents walking down aisle

28. Parents walking down aisle

29. Bridesmaids walking down aisle

30. Flower Girl & Ring Bearer walking down aisle

31. Bride and Dad walking down aisle (towards you)

32. Bride and Dad walking down aisle (away from you)

33. Dad giving away bride

34. Wide angle of ceremony

35. Readings

36. Vows

37. Other religious activities

38. Lighting of Unity Candle

39. Presentation of flowers to mothers

40. The kiss

41. Bride and Groom announced as husband and wife

42. Bride & Groom walking up the aisle

43. Bride & Groom kiss at end of aisle (Tell them to go hide now)

44. Wedding party couples walking up the aisle

45. Parents walking up aisle

After Ceremony

46. Bride & Groom kiss before they walk outdoors to crowd (silhouette shot)

47. Bride & Groom walk out to bubbles, bird seed, etc

———————————

(Back inside at altar)

48. Bride & Groom as a couple

49. Bride & Groom with Grandparents (Bride's Side #1)

50. Bride & Groom with Grandparents (Bride's Side #2)

51. Bride & Groom with Grandparents (Groom's Side #1)

52. Bride & Groom with Grandparents (Groom's Side #2)

53. Bride & Groom with Bride's Parents

54. Bride & Groom with Bride's Parents, Siblings

55. Bride & Groom with Bride's Parents, Siblings, Spouses, Children

56. Bride & Groom with Bride's Parents, Siblings, Spouses, Children, all extended family (including grandparents if they haven't left yet)

57. *Repeat the above shots if the Bride's parents are re-married

58. Bride & Groom with Groom's Parents

59. Bride & Groom with Groom's Parents, Siblings

60. Bride & Groom with Groom's Parents, Siblings, Spouses, Children

61. Bride & Groom with Groom's Parents, Siblings, Spouses, Children, all extended family (including grandparents if they haven't left yet)

61. *Repeat if the Groom's parents are re-married

—— dismiss the family to leave unless they are in the wedding party——

62. Bride & Groom with Maid of Honor and Best Man

63. Bride & Groom with Bridesmaids

64. Groom with Bridesmaids

65. Bride & Groom with wedding party

66. Bride & Groom with Groomsmen

67. Bride with Groomsmen

68. Bride and Groom together (Full length, half length, head and shoulders close-up)

69. Bride Alone

70. Groom Alone

71. Bride & Groom with Minister

---

72. Bride & Groom IN FRONT of party bus/limo

73. Bride & Groom INSIDE of party bus/limo

After Ceremony – Outdoors Location

74. Bride Alone

75. Groom Alone

76. Bride & Groom as a couple

77. Bride & Groom with Bridesmaids

78. Groom with Bridesmaids

79. Bride & Groom with wedding party

80. Bride & Groom with Groomsmen

81. Bride with Groomsmen

Reception

82. Cake (Take this first thing when you arrive at the reception. Cakes are known to fall over, so get it early.)

81. Wedding Party Entering

82. Bride & Groom entering

83. Wide-angle of head table

------Toast-----

84. Toast: Maid of Honor

85. Toast: Best Man

86. Toast: Bride & Groom

87. Toast: Bride & Groom close-up

88. Prayer (Just take one candid and don't be obnoxious about it.)

------After dinner-----

89. Bride & Groom close-up of rings with marriage license or flowers.

90. Candid Bride & Groom greeting guests at tables

------Cake-----

91. Bride & Groom cutting cake POSED

92. Bride & Groom cutting cake REAL

93. Bride & Groom feeding cake to each other

94. Bride & Groom kiss

95. Detail shots of cake, knife, cake on plate

------Dancing-----

96. Bride & Groom first dance POSED (Close-up half length)

97. Bride & Groom first dance CANDIDS (full length further away)

98. Wedding party dancing as couples POSED (Each couple)

99. Wedding party dancing as couples CANDID (wide-angle of group)

100. Father/daughter dance POSED

101. Father/daughter dance CANDIDs

102. Mother/son dance POSED

103. Mother/son dance CANDIDS

104. Other Festive Dances: Chair Dance, Dollar Dance, etc.

------Garter/bouquet-----

105. Bride holding bouquet POSED

106. Bride throwing bouquet

107. Groom holding garter POSED

108. Groom throwing garter

109. Bride & Groom with people who caught garter and bouquet

Special Requests

____

Notes (Take good notes of anything out of the ordinary. Example: the family was 2 hours late and you couldn't get any before pictures, etc. If there's something missing on your list, you need documentation why you missed it and what happened. Emotions run high at weddings and you might accidentally get blamed for something that was out of your control, so do the best job you can and keep good notes.)

DOUBLE CHECK this list is done and you've spoken with the Bride & Groom, and both sets of Parent's for any last requests.

7. THE SHORT VERSION ITINERARY

This is a shortened version of the detailed itinerary. This one is handy to print out and have your assistant keep in the clipboard until you get the hang of how long each of these sections usually lasts.

Pre-ceremony

- If you are starting at the church, begin 1 hour before the wedding.
- If you are starting at a different location, like the bride's home, then allow drive time, but you can really get all your pre-ceremony shots finished in an hour of photography time – provided the clients are ready to go. The run down is:

- Bride and her girls, and parents: 30 minutes
- Groom and his guys, and parents: 30 minutes

*A little trick: Figure your start time, and then tell everyone it's a half hour before that. Inevitably people WILL be late, however, they don't know the actual start time is a half hour later. Only the bride should know ...and the groom if he's the responsible-type.

Ceremony

- If it's a religious ceremony: 45 minutes – 1 hour.
- If it's NOT a religious ceremony: 15 – 20 minutes

After Ceremony

- Blowing Bubbles: 10 – 15 minutes
- At altar: 30 minutes to get all family, wedding party, bride and groom
- Leaving Church: 10 – 15 minutes
- Drive to second location: ______ minutes

Second Location

- Wedding Party with Bride and Groom: 30 minutes
- Drive to reception: ______ minutes

Reception

- Bride and Groom enter and get seated: 15-20 minutes
- Toast and other speakers: 15 minutes
- Dinner: 45 minutes – 1 hour
- Cake: 15 minutes
- Dancing: 1-2 hours
- Garter/Bouquet: 15 minutes

* * *

You'll be getting photo-journalistic and detail shots in between (when you're not doing the formal photographs) but these time frames give you a general itinerary of a well-organized wedding. You also have to communicate, ahead of time, how important it is for everyone to be ready to go in order to keep this schedule and keep things running smoothly. The faster the pictures go, the more time they get to spend with their guests and enjoy their special day.

8. YOUR DETAILED ITINERARY

Here's the run-down of how the day usually goes. If all else fails, and you forget something or lose this list, the most important thing to remember is just shoot like crazy, but hopefully that won't happen because you ARE a professional and remembered to pack all this stuff last night. However, if you find yourself in dire straits remember wedding days happen in a natural progression whether you have a shot list or not, so that will at least cover the "photojournalistic" stuff.

With everything being digital now, there's no reason to save shots because you might run out of film. It's nothing for me to shoot an average of one or two shots every minute for the entire day. Remember you can always edit them down later, but if you're unsure, it is better to shoot more now, than regret not getting something later. However, that being said, keep in mind what constant shooting will do to your battery power. In general I take two shots of each thing, unless I catch people blinking their eyes, then I take three. Anymore is overkill.

Throughout this itinerary, I'll use general terms for a Christian wedding. I've photographed weddings of different faiths, and while each one is slightly different, they all are about the same idea. A couple that enters into a mutual contract that invites their family and friends to share in the event. That being said, I will use generic terms like altar, church, minister, groom - his, bride - hers, etc. – but know that these terms and pronouns can be substituted as needed. The point is – as long as you respect your surroundings and this special day for your clients, it doesn't matter what kind of wedding you are photographing, you will be prepared.

One Week Before

At this point you should already have all of your paper work together: contract, diving directions, and shot list. It's a good idea to call the church a week before the wedding and talk to the minister or whoever coordinates weddings and discuss their rules for photography.

The rules are pretty standard of most churches, sometimes it is up to the individual minister, but until you do enough weddings to remember who likes what, it's a good idea to know these rules in advance. For example, I found out the hard way that in New York City, Trinity Church at the end of Wall St, only allows one photographer.. period. I was relieving a different photographer and there was an overlap of about 10 minutes. I started shooting early to give the bride some variety and then out of nowhere I actually had some guy come up to me a rip my camera out of my hands. I was completely shocked and certainly not expecting this kind of aggression. To this day I'm still not sure if he was even affiliated with the church, but it was clear even though I thought I knew the rules of this venue, apparently I did not... or maybe this guy didn't know that I was the official photographer. In St Louis, MO: The Old Cathedral (The one by the Arch) does not allow any sort of flash system at all, at any point. The Daniel Boone Chapel (in Defiance, MO) does not allow wheeled vehicles to the chapel. It's a historical site – meaning you have to hike it about a ¼ mile from the parking lot to get your gear to the church. St. Louis University College Church does NOT have parking for you – you have to feed the meter in the middle of the ceremony... yes, I'm serious. The point is, call ahead. *Know before you go.*

You should also have received all of your payments from your client. This is very typical of wedding services. Most every wedding vendor requires full payment before the date.

Do a gear check. Make sure all of your equipment is functioning properly. In St. Louis, you can rent things from Schiller's in a pinch.

The Day Of – LET'S DO THIS!!!

You should arrive AT LEAST 1.5 hours before the wedding. Sometimes I'll get there 2 hours prior. The worst thing would be arriving late. Give yourself plenty of time. You never know what will happen, construction, an accident, you realize you have to get gas, there are two Marriott's and each one is on the other side of town, you get lost, etc. Getting there early also gives you a chance to do some recon on your location. Look for trees and shady spots, stairways, archways, etc. These will be your backgrounds if you choose not to use a backdrop. (I don't like to use backdrops unless necessary.)

Find the outlets in the church. Usually they have at least one in the chapel close to the alter within the first 5 pews or along the sidewalls. (This is where you will plug in your soft-box later. Now is also a good to find out where your outlets are before the chaos begins.) Put your stuff in the last back pew so nobody sits there. Put your tripods, light stands, and soft-box under the pew. This is your ideal "base" during the ceremony. Sometimes you can find outlets back there too and use them to charge up your gear.

At this point, you might run into the florist. They are usually there putting flowers on the pews, but not usually more than one hour beforehand. This is a good time to introduce yourself with a smile. Give a business card, make small talk - something like, "Do you know the bride and groom personally? Are you going to the reception as well? Do you do a lot of weddings? These flowers look amazing!" The idea is to build a relationship. If they are a business, you will more than likely run into them again and it is important to make friends with other vendors.

Wedding Events are like any other job. Successful photographers network, and when Brides book other wedding vendors, they oftentimes ask the florist, DJ, etc., if they know of any good photographers. This is also a good time to ask the florist about the boutonnieres, corsages and such.

Tell the florist you are going to be taking the formal pictures in about 5 minutes and ask if there's anything you can do to help with getting the flowers where they need to go. You might be saying to yourself, "yeah, but that's not the photographers job", but the real question is, "Do you want to leave your schedule up to other people with their own agendas?" – Of course you don't. Taking charge of these small things enable your itinerary to stay on schedule and also a good PR move.

Turn your phone on vibrate but keep it with you. When you arrive at the wedding venue, at some point, find the coordinator and minister. Check in with both of them. Introduce yourself.

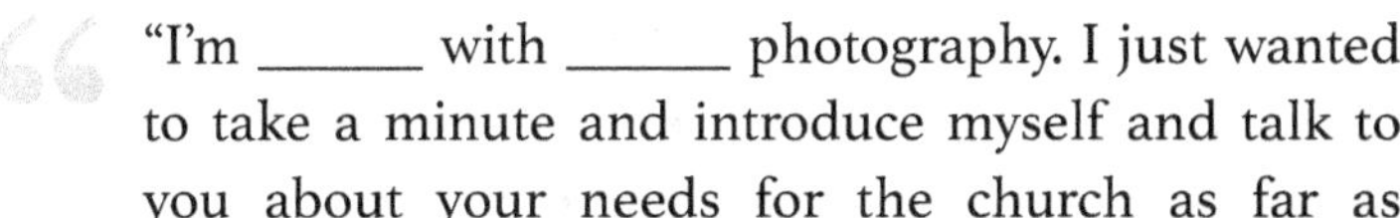
"I'm _______ with _______ photography. I just wanted to take a minute and introduce myself and talk to you about your needs for the church as far as

restrictions and so forth. I also want you to know that I fully respect this as a place of worship and not a photography studio so I am fully prepared to follow the guidelines you have for photographing. (Try not to say, "Shooting," say "photographing". We use "shooting" between ourselves but it is rather offensive to non-photographers.) If it's ok with you, I usually only use flash while they are coming down the aisle, and I *never* come more than half way up the aisle. I will NOT use flash during any point of the ceremony. If we are allowed to take photos after the wedding at the altar, I can get everything done in a half hour. How does that sound?"

By this point, you might get a dropped jaw from the coordinator or minister. They are not used to such professionalism; so by just taking a minute to do this not only gets you on their good side, but it also makes them want to work with you in the future. This is a very important PR move that's a win-win for everyone and might get you more work later. It is really nice for a minister to have you on his/her "preferred" photographer list.

While you are exploring the ceremony area and looking for electrical outlets, take an ambient light reading up at the altar. If the minister is nearby, ask him if he knows if there will be any additional lights during the ceremony, or if the current lighting is how it will be. It's ok if not, you're going to use a tripod anyway. Also you might want to skip asking this if the minister is grumpy.

Now go find the bride. They usually have her in a back room somewhere so the groom can't see her. If no one is around yet, find the nursery. Sometimes they put bridal parties in there. Make sure to knock as the women are probably dressing. I always knock and crack the door open and say, Hi, it's the photographer, Is everyone decent?"

When you go in, greet the bride with a smile. Don't ask her if she's nervous, it will only make it worse. Be calm, relaxed, and chill. This will help ease her tension too. Start out something like this,

> "Hi _______. Well, I'm just checking in for a minute. I'm going to let you girls get situated and then in a few minutes I'll come back and we'll get you and your bridesmaids and you girls getting ready. Also if you have the dress here, I'd like to take a few pictures of it on the hanger before you put it on."

(This prompts them to get a move on it if they've been dilly-dallying).

Remember you're the orchestrator for the most part, and since you will have already discussed the itinerary prior to the wedding day, she will know what to expect. This is also a good time to determine if you need to go get your backdrop. If it's decent looking, you'll be doing mid-length shots anyway and you won't see too much of the background. However if it's in a nursery, and there are elephants on the wall, and you might want the backdrop and the light. Don't worry if you don't have one, you can try to pull them away from the wall and get the background to fall out of focus. If you can find a fake tree or plant, even better. Feel free to move things around, but make sure to put things back where you found them too. Another tip: if the bride has a long big poufy dress with a train, you can have a few of the bridesmaids hold the back of it up behind the bride as a makeshift background. You're going to be half-length to close-up anyway so you won't be able to tell in the picture. Obviously, don't do this in front of a window because she will only have the crinoline underneath (in case you're unfamiliar, that's the netting slip.)

Go find the groom. The groomsmen usually don't arrive at the same time as the bride. All they have to do is throw their tuxes on, and they don't take as long as the girls to get ready, so it's not uncommon for them to arrive much later than the bride.

Same thing, introduce yourself. Keep in mind that the guys usually don't care too much about the photography. They just want to get it over with so they can party. When you're talking with the groom, tell him you've already spoken with the bride and you are going to get a few of the girls getting ready, but you'll be back shortly to get the guys getting ready so if he can, try to get him to get his guys together and dressed. Assure him that you know those things (tuxedos) are uncomfortable and that you'll get him and his guys done as soon as humanly possible. Ask if his parents are there because you'll want to get them too.

This is also a good time to remind him to tell his groomsmen that right after the wedding they will have to *jet* upfront to the altar for pictures, so no going to the cars and stuff just yet because you're only allowed a half hour to get it all done.

Tell him "If we can get everyone on the same page, we'll get through these pics lightning quick. The faster we get the pictures done, the faster you guys can get to the party".

Tell him when you come back you'll photograph him, his best man, his groomsmen, and mom and dad and that the they should also have on their boutonnieres, but you can help with that if they don't know how to do it.

Go back to the bride's area. Photograph her dress on the hanger or over the chair. Basically, everything you photograph will follow the format of: full-length, mid-length, and close-up. This includes details of things like the dress, shoes, flowers, and jewelry in the box. Think of what would be in a magazine ad pic. For example: Full length of dress on the hanger including the whole door, and then close-up details of the buttons, beading, etc.

While you're doing this tell the girls in the room that as soon as they're ready, you'll start with them. Tell them they will need their flowers and jewelry on if they don't have them already. They don't even have to put on their shoes, for this part you'll be doing mid-length anyway.

You'll be photographing them individually with the bride from half length, so as soon as a few girls have been done, have them go fetch mom and dad and tell them dad needs his boutonniere and mom her corsage.

After you're done photographing the girls and the bride's parents, head back over and do the same set of shots for the groom's side. If someone is not ready, just wait. Don't run back and forth between bride and groom. It will start you off on the wrong tone all day and then the pics will look out of sync for postproduction later.

Stand your ground if you can. Sometimes you'll be missing someone and they'll say, it's OK we can just get that shot later, you can go back to the grooms side." This is when you politely say, "Well, that idea is good in theory, but it's been my experience that with all the confusion and busyness of the day, we probably won't get that opportunity later. I can wait a few more minutes.

After you've done the pre-ceremony pics, go back to base at the last pew and check your gear. Battery level? CF card? Phone on vibrate? Go through your checklist, and cross off what you've done so far, and look for any special pre-ceremony requests that you may have missed. This is also a good time to revisit the contract and memorize again the names of mom, and dad.

Also look for post ceremony special request, bubbles, and the dreaded-receiving line. The receiving line is a terrible idea and I'll explain why. Talk them out of it at all costs. They will see their guests at the reception anyway. After the bride and groom finish eating at the reception is the best time for them to receive their guests, not after the wedding. I can't stress this enough because having a receiving line after the ceremony could replace your only time for family pictures.

Sometimes they will say, "Oh that's ok we'll just get the family pics at the reception". Again, ...terrible idea. I don't blame then for thinking this would be logical, but here again, you are the professional, you do this just about every weekend, and there are a million reasons why you have set this itinerary to run in this order. Here are just a few:

Once you get to the reception it is rude to the other guests, that are not family, to have to sit through this.

Nobody looks good after they've stuffed their faces with dinner, or have had more than a few drinks.

It's nearly impossible to get everyone together at the same time again; somebody's in the bathroom, at the bar, out in the car, changing diapers, out smoking, someone left for good, etc.

There are usually no stairs like up at an alter for you to stack large families so you end up with people sitting on the floor and it's not flattering.

The lighting is usually bad. Ok enough for now ...you get the point.

Back to the ceremony.

When the girls are lined up at the back of the church go back and give them the quick tutorial of how to walk. Tell them they do not need to stop. Just keep walking, unless something terrible goes wrong and you give the 'wait just a minute gesture.' But don't hold them up too long. Don't stop the wedding just for this – you can always get them again coming back up the aisle after the ceremony if you have to. Anyway, you will have pre-focused on a pew that's at the same spot as the girls will be when you take the shot. This 'pre-focus' trick also works well for sneaky candid pics at the reception and other times. Don't trust the auto-focus for the aisle shots. You only get one chance at the aisle shots and there's no room for error or auto-focus camera delay.

It's also ok, and expected of you, to be in the aisle for this, don't worry. However, it is smart, and classy, of you to quickly step back into the closest pew as wedding guests in the front will also be taking photos and you never know when you might have a camera fail and need one of those guest's photos. It's never happened to me, but it's happened to some of my colleagues. Having guests over your shoulder taking your posed shots is annoying, but unavoidable and they may save you're @%$ some day so try not to be a snobby photographer.

During the ceremony stay near the back of the church. It's ok for you to set up your tripod right in the middle of the back of aisle during this time. You might have a problem with uncle Joe and his camcorder tripod but hopefully you can work around it, or if you have to, quietly ask him if he could move it in the pew a bit more so it won't be in your shot.

If they do a unity candle or flowers to the mothers, sometimes the minister will let you use flash, but don't count it, and it has to be pre-arranged with them before the ceremony. I usually don't even bother; I just take it without flash. They will at least hold still for a few seconds so they don't spill hot wax on themselves and there is a slight pause for a hug for flower presentation, and that's usually enough time for you to take a steady shot even without flash as long as you're using a tripod.

Immediately after the ceremony. You only have a **half hour** to do all the family, wedding party, and bride & groom shots right after the ceremony, try as best as you can to convince them NOT to do a receiving line. (This should have already been discussed before the wedding so there are no surprises.) This includes the kind where the bride and groom release the pews/rows of guests. This also includes them greeting people at the back of the church. It is vital that the bride and groom exit as soon as possible and then either run around the back of the church or hide in the limo if it's an outside wedding and they have nowhere to go.

Let the guest exit normally. If they are going to do bubbles or something like that, then that's fine but you need to make the bride and groom aware that in order for all this to run both smoothly and efficiently then they need to trust you on this. If they want to do bubbles or butterfly release, or something, instruct the guests exit normally and wait outside then close the doors and wait for you. (The bride and groom should be hiding while the guests exit.) Also this is a tender first moment for them as husband and wife and since you will be at the back of the exit anyway, you might want to snap a few candid shots of them alone together without them seeing you, plus it's a nice time for them to have a quiet moment together before the obligated craziness of the rest of the day.

After the bride and groom come out of hiding, tell them to wait for your queue before they exit through the bubble or bird seed archway, take a few shots of them at the foot of the steps with the guests blowing bubbles, etc. This can make a super silhouette shot.

Then you pass the bride and groom and go outside and position yourself in the middle of the walkway. (You might have to tell the crowd to, on queue, start blowing bubbles like crazy, or throw birdseed, or whatever they have.) Then, when you're ready, have the bride and groom walk through and immediately go around the back and straight up to the alter.

While the crowd is still outside, this is when you say with gusto, "Attention please, we need all members of the immediate and extended family to come back in and sit near the front of the church, after the third or fourth pew for some quick photos. You should know who you are. (Only call on family they've decided beforehand they want in the pictures.) Tell them you will do Grandparents first so that they can leave first.

This might all sound a little strict, but we see it all the time, and the same thing always happens when the bride and groom hang around at the back of the church after the ceremony where people can see them. It automatically turns into at least a 30-45 minute receiving line and then there goes your time slot for pictures.

Inform your clients that there will be plenty of time at the reception for the bride and groom to go around and greet the tables, (the bride and groom usually go table-to-table right after they finish eating because they will get done eating before everyone else and this is the perfect time for them to do this).

In the meantime, tell your client that it is imperative that all the immediate family know that they are expected to be ready immediately following the ceremony for pictures...this means - for them- no going to the car to pack stuff up, running to QuikTrip, etc. This may sound a bit drill sergeant-ish but they will thank you later when the guests don't have to wait at the reception, and everyone gets the pictures they want in a timely manner.

Of course, they will have the final say. If they really want to do a receiving line, that's their choice. It IS their wedding, they will just have to understand that having a receiving line may mean that they miss out on pictures. You cannot be a superhero. You can only do what you can do, in a short amount of time, and that's why it's so important to have these details worked out ahead of time.

While you are outside getting the bubbles pics, have your assistant take your equipment up to the front of the church and set it about three pews back. Have he/she set up your Soft-box, (about 3 or 4 rows back at a 45° from the alter depending on the strength of your light source), connect the radio transmitter and connect the power cord to the power supply to the closest outlets.

If you don't have an assistant, then you'll have to hustle back and do it yourself. As the family members meander in, have them sit anywhere after the third or fourth row so they don't knock over your equipment and their heads are not in the side of the wide angle shots. It's also a good idea to set your tripod right in the middle of the aisle at the third row. This helps prevent people from wandering up to close and keeps them out of your way.

After the ceremony the guest photographers will be almost on top of you with their snap and shoot cameras. The worst is after the wedding up at the alter for family pics. The best way to handle this is, after you get your first group posed, you'll see the swarm of point and shoot cameras snapping away. You politely say with a jovial tone. "Ok everybody, I don't mind if you take photos, take all you want, but let me get my shot first. If I can, I'll even give you a queue when to take yours if time allows. The point is these lovely people are paying me to be here and I don't want them blinking in my pictures. Deal? You all just be ready when I say go." They might laugh, but usually this gets a handle on that problem.

After you take two or three shots say, "Ok fan-club, your turn," and do this for each group. Don't be afraid to fluff their feathers if they start slowing you down. If it gets real bad, just ignore them and get your job done. When the peanut gallery starts to complain, apologize and inform them that we just don't have much time left and they WILL kick you out of a church. Trust me on this. Catholic churches are the most strict about it. They will turn the lights off on you. I'm not kidding.

This will be the craziest part of your day, but don't worry; you'll be done in a half hour and already halfway through the day. This is the only part of the day that the assistant might work harder than you do and if you don't have an assistant, then you are a super trooper and I commend you.

You will basically pose the bride and groom on the center step of the alter. You will add and subtract family members and wedding party as needed. The bride and groom pretty much stay put the whole time.

Start with the grandparents and families, so they can leave first. Then the wedding party so they can start to gather things up and get things ready for the next location, then the bride and groom. This will be the fastest part of the day, but if you stick to the Real Shot List it will be cake.

Whoever has the clipboard should go through and make sure you've got all the family pics they want. There's no time to do it later. I have done remainder family pics at a reception, but I would not recommend it, as it usually never goes well.

Now is also good to take a pic of the marriage license signing if they have it ready, but not all couples want this.

Double check home-base (under the pew) to make sure you didn't leave anything behind. Pack your stuff and jet to the car.

On your way to the car, introduce yourself to the driver of the bus or trolley – again a good PR move and you will need to follow him and don't want him to lose you in traffic. Even though you have your schedule, it's nothing for them to veer of course and stop at a gas station or bar. If you make friends with the driver, he'll keep an eye out for you while driving.

At the next location, you will repeat the wedding party group shots, and the bride and groom couple shots, but with different poses. The families do not come to the second location. Occasionally the flower girl, and ring bearer will, but this isn't typical either. It usually depends on their age and how they're acting that day. It's not a big deal because you already have it at the church anyway.

You'll do the same series of photos as you did at the alter except these are more fun in nature – not so stiff and formal. Also it's very likely the wedding party had some alcohol on their trolley and might be a bit rambunctious. The groomsmen might protest and be grumpy because at this point they are starting to sweat in their tuxes. This is when you remind them that the faster we all get this done, the faster they can get to the party.

For these shots it's a general rule for them not to be holding cigarettes and beer in the group shots unless the bride wants it. You have to remember the bride's parents traditionally pay for these pictures and the parents of the bride and groom don't want to see pictures of their little angels like that, much less have to pay for them – Besides, the girls in the wedding party might be taking snapshots of this anyway. Now if they request that you go to a bar for one of the locations, then obviously, this is something that is important to them so oblige accordingly.

Once you are done, go over and talk to the driver. Tell him you want to get a head start so that you can be at the reception and ready to take photos as soon as they pull up. Again, if you've done your PR work, he will work with you on this, unless he's on an hourly limit, then just do the best you can. You may have to park behind the driver when you pull up to reception, get the shot coming out of the limo, and then go park your car, but don't worry because the DJ will spend a few minutes or so with the wedding party in the vestibule of the reception hall going over the itinerary for the night and most of the wedding party will be using the restrooms at this time. This buys you about 10 minutes to get situated.

At the reception, as soon as possible find a table. If it's a place-setting deal, hopefully you've already discussed your meal requirements before hand and will have a place setting. If not, it's smart to team up with the DJ.

More PR work – Introduce yourself to the DJ with a smile, by this time you should be a pro at this. Hand him your card and tell him they've only got you for the major stuff – toast, cake, dances, garter bouquet- and ask what his schedule for the night looks like. This is the most important vendor relationship besides the minister. Up until now, you were the orchestrator of the day. Now the ball is in the DJ's court. This DJ could make your life bliss, or make it a living hell. If you get on his good side, you can coordinate when he's announcing events, and he will make sure you are in place before he does anything. If you are on his bad side, you might miss things like the dance, cake, toast, anything. It's a good idea to consider the DJ your partner in crime for the night. If you have a table, invite him to sit with you for dinner. He might just stay at his booth, but the offer creates an unspoken unity; that you both are equal and are working together on this job. This is also the vendor that which you will spend the most time. If you continue doing weddings you most likely will work with him again. Also DJs and Photographers go hand-n-hand. DJs get clients all the time asking them if they know any good photographers, and DJs like to promote people that they enjoy working with; being that you spend the majority of the evening with him.

At all of the reception events, position yourself for the best shot. You're not in the church anymore. The DJ doesn't care if you're blocking his view. If people get in your way for things like the cake cutting, dances, etc. don't be afraid to be obnoxious and say "Excuse me. I need to stand there." Obviously don't do this for the prayer or the toasts, but you get my point.

After the toast there might be a prayer, photograph this but don't be obnoxious about it or come in for a close-up.

Now go put your camera down because you are going to sneak in line to eat. After the bride, groom and the wedding party go through the line, **wait for the parents to go through**, then jump in right AFTER the parents. You can even look at the next one in line and say, 'Do you mind if I jump in here?' This is very common for photographers, but feels weird the first time you do it. This is acceptable practice because you need to be finished eating at the same time the bride and groom finish eating so you can be ready when they need you.

After you are finished eating, go talk to the bride and groom. This will most likely be the only time the rest of the night that they are together without having planned festivities. Tell them this is a good time to do the pic with the bouquet and the rings and hands. They don't even have to move, you can take it right there at their table, just turn their chairs around, place their hands together with the flowers in the background and shoot down so the bride's dress is the background. This is a close up, so tell them to close their eyes. You don't want them to be blinded by your flash. When you're done with that, instruct them that this is a good time for them to greet their guests from table to table because they won't get a chance to do it later.

While they are receiving and greeting their guests, take a few candid shots, but don't get people stuffing their face with food – it's unflattering. Go to a few tables and say, "Excuse me, do you mind if I get a quick group photo?" Have half the table come around and stand behind the seated guests. (Only take a few of these, not ALL the tables, as it will take up the rest of the night.)

Go check in with the DJ and see when the other things will start. The next event is usually the cake.

Most of the events will be photographed as it happens, but you should stage a close shot right before so at least you get one good one. This is important especially with the cake, and garter/bouquet toss.

Go find the cake knife and the serving utensil. If it's not over by the cake already, ask the caterers for it. Tell them you need it for pictures.

Instruct the bride and groom to wait for your queue so you can get a posed one first.

After you are done with the major stuff, hang out for a while. It's not a good idea to partake in the alcohol. Remember other eyes are watching you. It is completely unprofessional to drink on the job. The bride and groom might even insists, but politely tell them you might join the festivities only after you are finished and your stuff is packed away.

Go through your checklist again. Triple check you've got everything on that list. If not, go to the bride and tell her what you're missing. Don't just assume she'll forget because she won't and they might use that as a reason to try and get money back from you later.

Address what you are missing and decide together if it's feasible to recreate it. She will probably be exhausted by that point and not want to do it anyway, but you still need to ask. Tell the couple that you have everything you need and that you will stick around for a bit in case they think of something, but if not, that it was a pleasure working with them and you'll call them in about two weeks if not sooner.

Now go to the parents and say the same thing, and maybe add that you do family portraits as well, if they ever need someone. They will be elated that you worked so hard, and kept your cool, and stayed on track, that they will most definitely refer you to other people... And that's how your successful business as a wedding photographer all starts.

9. JUST SHOWING UP

Before you even get to the 'Big Day' there's a ton of prep work to be done. This includes a few meetings with the bride and groom, and a few phone calls to the other vendors. If you're feeling that this is unnecessary, I'd like to start off with some empathy building to help paint the picture of why this prep work is so important. You may be tempted to think sure, I could mosey in the day of and just photograph what happens as the day goes, but here's what that looks like in a nutshell.

"Hi, I'm the photographer. Who are you?"

"I'm the pastor. Look, I don't like photographers who make a big scene, just stay out of my way and don't be obvious."

"Um, ok. Where's the bride?"

"How should I know I just got here. Also there's another wedding right after this so you have to be done with everything in 30 minutes."

"Um.. ok do you know where anyone else is?"

"No"

...you spend the next 15-20 minutes running around looking for people. You now have a half hour left to take all the 'before pics' on that 15 page list of 'must-have shots' the bride gave you two days ago. You finally find the bride. Surprise! She's not ready. Also the florist hasn't arrived yet, so nobody has his or her flowers. Most of the bridesmaids are still in jeans and yoga pants.

"I'd like to get started with the photography, but I see we are still missing people. I'll go find the groom. Is he here yet?"

"Umm. I don't know. I haven't seen him since yesterday. Kate (Groom's sister) is Brad here yet?"

"No, they were out late for the bachelor party and probably won't be here till a few minutes before."

"Uh ok so what do you want me to take pictures of?"

"Umm well if you can wait a few minutes the girls are going to help me get into my dress and..."

20 more minutes go by. You now have 5 minutes to get ALL of your 'before pictures.'

Can you begin to see how one small glitch can lead to another? The whole thing snowballs and before you know it you've lost control. You no longer have a professional handle on the day's schedule and are scrambling to play catch up with everything for rest of the day. Here's where I'll add the stress of all this.

Weddings only happen once. There are no redo's. If you mess up and couldn't deliver on what you promised the client, it is very likely you will get sued. At the very least your reputation will be tarnished because the bride will make sure to tell everyone she knows how horrible the experience was. Remember that saying? A thankful client might tell one person, but an angry client will tell anyone who will listen.

In the upcoming chapters I have everything set out for you in a checklist type fashion. I'll include links in the appendix where you can use direct downloads to the lists so you can edit and print them off if you wish.

You're Welcome.

10. 'WE CAN JUST GET IT LATER!'

This is a follow up to the Detailed Itinerary, and an ode to when the bride says, "Oh, we're out of time here? It's ok we'll just get the rest of the family pictures at the reception!". This never works...ever. Why not?

1. Nobody looks good after sweating all day and then eating a big meal.
2. Everyone scatters at the reception. It's hard enough to get the bride and groom together for shots, let alone an entire family...
3. 'But wait! We can have the DJ make an announcement.' Sure, you could,...but then Aunt Susie is in the bathroom, Uncle Bobby is outside having a smoke,... 20 minutes go by with the rest of the group standing there posed and giving you the evil eye because none of this is working out like they thought it would.
4. Reception halls don't make for good backgrounds and the lighting is dreadful.
5. Most people are 'letting-loose' and celebrating, meaning

they have already taken off their jackets, loosened their ties, unbuttoned collars, may have spilled something , or changed into other clothes, etc.

6. The flowers look sad and wilted by this time of the night.

11. THE PRO WEDDING WARRIOR KIT

Before you start photographing wedding professionally, you need to act the part and look the part. This includes arming yourself with the proper supplies besides just your camera. Following is the ultimate list for your PRO kit.

PART I

GENERAL SUPPLIES

1. A clean full size white bed sheet – use this for the bride to sit on outside so she doesn't get dirty
2. White chalk – This hides dirt scuffs on the bride's dress
3. Unscented Baby wipes (travel pouch of 10 is plenty) – cleans just about any mess quickly
4. Safety pins – for 'wardrobe malfunctions'
5. Bobby pins – for flyaway hair
6. A few rubber bands
7. Duct tape
8. A few paper towels or tissues in a sandwich baggy
9. Bug spray
10. A pair of black socks – Maybe for you and/or a drunk groomsmen that falls into a fountain
11. Sewing kit
12. An umbrella – try to get a nice looking one maybe with printed flowers - you may end up using it as a prop

13. A professional looking bag of some sort to hold all this
     stuff, as you will be using it for every wedding - a luggage
     tote works best
14. Some quarters in case you need to pay a meter

PART II

———

THE ASSISTANT

Having an assistant will make your day so much easier. The assistant's job is to help you with moving equipment around the locations, gathering the necessary family and wedding members for upcoming pictures, holding reflectors, and for checking off your shot-list; which we will cover later.

The assistant should have a clipboard (get one with a compartment) that holds the shot-list on top and inside have the event paperwork: contract, directions, a wedding program or any other stationary or wedding items they hand out at the wedding (bubbles, petals, etc.)

PART III

SUPPLIES FOR THE PHOTOGRAPHER AND ASSISTANT

1. A great attitude
2. Your shot list, contract, and driving directions – yes even if you have your GPS print them out anyway
3. Your fully charged camera and EMPTY CF cards- obviously
4. Your flash
5. Your tripod
6. A reflector
7. Light meter
8. Multi-tool or Swiss army knife
9. Flash Diffuser
10. Radio transmitter for lights
11. Up to 2 photo umbrellas or Softbox lights with stands, but 1 powerful light will be plenty and is easier to transport
12. A backdrop and 2 stands if you have it
13. Extra CF cards
14. Extra batteries

15. Power cord – I like the long orange industrial cords - affix your address label around it so the venue doesn't assume it belongs to them

16. 3-prong to 2-prong converter for the end of your cord – Many older venues will only have two-prong outlets where you need to plug in your light, so this little adapter is worth its weight in gold

17. A wheeled luggage bag - you can find some dark foam inserts to make separators inside for your gear or look at any department store in the closet organizer section

18. A clipboard for your assistant (Even if he/she is just scribbling, it makes everything look more official).

19. Pens or pencils

20. A cooler with an ice pack

21. Water (Even if its just one, you can refill it at the venue at the water fountain)

22. Snacks (fruit, chips, etc. – stuff that won't melt in your car)

23. Real Food – No one like a grumpy photographer. Sub sandwiches are good in the event that you don't get a break, you can eat in the car while you're driving to the next location.

24. Toy squeaker – You may have to do surgery on a stuffed animal or dog toy to get your hands on one of these, but you can use them to deal with unruly children when it comes time to take family portraits. Hide it in the palm of your hand and tell them you know magic. Then press on their shoe at the same time you press the hidden squeaker. Their eyes will grow wide with wonderment and you will have their attention for the rest of the day. Tell the grownups to **watch the camera** – not you, so that when the moment strikes you are ready to fire the shutter and the adults are not looking at the children, looking at you, in all the images.

25. Business cards

26. Event website cards (see if you can place these around other wedding stuff such as the guest-book - that is if someone brought it over from the ceremony - maybe the gift table - maybe by the cake table - but don't make it obvious) Wait until they **serve** the cake to place the cards on this table because people will be coming up at their leisure to get cake and it's not so intrusive as placing before the cake is cut - plus it's just respectful for whomever made the cake. The company may want to put their own cards out so they should have the best real estate for card placement since it is *their* product you are wanting to place your cards next to.

27. Also print out an email sign-up sheet – if you are posting the proofs to a website later. *some post-production sites have these sheets for you to print out from their website for free. You might try asking the bartenders if you can place the email sheet up at the bar. *Don't forget to drop a tip in their jar if they say yes.

12. EXPOSURES AND LIGHTING

Most of the time I will take a light reading just to make sure of exposures. However, after doing this a while, and considering most Christian weddings are at 2pm, starting an hour or so before the ceremony, between May and October, you begin to see a trend in light adjustments and a recurring theme for exposure settings. It might be a good idea to jot down some of your favorite settings for pocket reference. If all else fails use auto, but it's a good idea to practice getting used to manual settings as the camera doesn't always know what you want it to do. This is where the phrase 'You have to know the rules to break the rules' comes into play. If you become the master of manual camera adjustments you can manipulate the image *exactly* how you want it and create some really unique and interesting imagery just by altering composition and lighting choices.

OUTDOOR LIGHTING
DURING THE DAY

The best time for outdoor photography is the golden hour; about an hour before dusk and an hour after dawn, but you will most likely be shooting at high noon so you have to be creative with outdoor ambient lighting the day of.

In the past I used a flash while outdoors, but now I only use flash outdoors if I am stuck in direct sun or the shade spot is splotchy. Otherwise, find some nice thick shade where there will be no uneven shadows on the face. Full shade is great.

When you are beginning you might think full sun is the best, but this lighting is really harsh so if your subject has wrinkles, or any imperfections, it will amplify these characteristics. You could also get stuck in the trap of raccoon-shadow-eyes. This happens when the sun is directly above and cast harsh shadow pockets in the eye sockets. Do yourself a favor and stick to thick shade. The one exception to this is an overcast day. This is actually the most perfect lighting for portraits. The thick clouds in the sky act as a giant Softbox or Umbrella for the sun and diffuses the light evenly; which creates nice soft even lighting.

I usually do not use outdoor flash because:

- outdoor flash can look fake.
- using outdoor flash is just a quicker way for you to drain your battery
- if you use outdoor flash on one grouping and not the other, then the pictures won't match and it will look like something went wrong.

You have to remember that your gear has high demands put on it this day and you NEED the flash at the reception, you DO NOT NEED the flash outside during the day. Some photographers still insist on using flash outside and that's fine. These are just the reasons I don't use it anymore unless necessary, and by necessary I mean - the only shaded area places splotchy spots on the faces and for some weird reason your assistant can't use a reflector to block the spots. It's just better in this instance to keep things 'au natural' if possible.

You have to remember that weddings are a whole different ball game. It's not a magazine shoot or a studio session where you get the luxury of taking your time and having all of your equipment on hand in a permanent spot. You are essentially a mobile studio and you have to get it done on the fly, yet still be professional.

There's so much to keep track of. You need to be as efficient as possible. Less is more here - so back to work.

You want to expose for their face. I take a light reading within an inch of their cheek. Your subject might be inquisitive and ask, 'what's that?' If they are a fun bunch, you can jokingly say, 'you are testing for signs of intelligent life.'

Outside sunny can be F8 at 125th, or higher F11 at 125th or really sunny at F16 at 250th. If you're shooting at that I feel your pain, your bride and groom probably are having problems opening their eyes because it's so bright out.

A trick for blinkers and bright sun is to tell them to close their eyes and open their eyes on the count of three. On three, you will take the picture. You can also take advantage of the reflector here. Bounce in some light on their dark side. You will either need your assistant for this, or a reflector stand, or Aunt Betty from the photo fan-club mentioned earlier. You can also use the reflector to hold over the bride and groom to block splotchy shade spots.

INDOOR WINDOW LIGHT

This can be some really beautiful lighting. Pose the person right next to the window so that the window light falls on only one side of their face and body. You might want to have your assistant bounce some light in with a reflector for the other darker side so there is not such a harsh contrast between the sun side and the shadow side. If you are 'sans' assistant. Try using bounce flash and drag the shutter a 1/30th of a second. This can be tricky on the fly so take a few different lighting options and edit down to the best lighting choice post production.

North sided windows are most evenly lit throughout the day as far as color temperature, so be aware of this if you had planned on using the same window at different times of the day. I usually try to have different backgrounds for each set of images so you don't have to worry about this.

CHURCH DURING CEREMONY

If it's a dark church I'll shoot around F4 at ¼ second, NO flash. You might be saying that's nuts, you'll get motion blur. Of course with these settings you will be using a tripod and the reason why this exposure still works is that ceremonies are usually really slow in movement. Remember the history of photography? Back in the day people had to hold still for lengthy amounts of time for portraits. The digital SLR cameras function the same way as a film camera. As long as there is not a lot of movement, you can still get surprisingly clear images. You have the tripod, so that takes care of you not moving. The bride and groom are paused for a few seconds for each of these shots during the ceremony, so that's just enough time for it to work. I'm not saying there won't be ANY motion blur but you can edit later, and you can't use flash anyway during the ceremony so you might as well make the best of it and get some gorgeous ambient light from the surrounding area. Of course, every church is different so take a light reading just before the ceremony to get your best exposure, or use auto exposure if you don't have a light meter, or are in a pinch.

OUTSIDE LATE AFTERNOON OR EARLY EVENING

This will be the toughest as you will need to adjust your setting probably every 10 minutes or more the closer you get to sunset. Start out around F8 at 125th or less. Don't be a hero and guess here. You don't have time. Trust your meter, take frequent readings, or have your assistant take them. If all else fails use auto.

*If you really want to nerd-out and plan things down to the minute, you can find out the time of sunset and plan around that with a sunset calculator. Just plug in your own date, and location: http://www.timeanddate.com/worldclock/astronomy.html?n=605

INDOOR RECEPTION

This will be the easiest. Set it and forget it at F5.6 at a 30th. Use bounce flash (unless there are really tall ceilings, then use normal flash with a diffuser). You might be saying, "That's crazy! A 30th of a second will be blurry with people dancing and what not!" The reason why this exposure works is because of the flash. Yes, a 30th is slow, but **the flash freezes any motion** right as the shutter opens and you get gorgeous warm ambient light from the remainder of the 30th. This setting never fails you as long as your flash is working properly. Some people do F8 at a 60th. That's OK too, it's a safe setting, but your background will be darker and the ambient colors aren't as nice.

MY EXPOSURES DISCLAIMER

These suggested exposures are just what I use. Please don't take them for guaranteed perfect photography.

Photography is its own science. Practice, practice, practice. Over time you will find the settings that are right for you.

13. QUICK AND STEALTHY
POSING TIPS

Here are a few pointers on how to quickly pose people so that the final result is more flattering.

For Women

Have them stand so that their feet are shaped like a 'T' with the front foot pointed at the camera and the back foot is perpendicular. Have them shift all their weight on the back foot so that the front leg relaxes. This instantly gives the entire body a super model 'S' curve shape and works for any body type. It doesn't even matter if they have a big skirt and you can't see their legs. It still works and minimizes appearance at the waist.

I usually say this as an announcement when I'm posing the first big family portrait up at the alter after the ceremony so that everyone can hear it. Announcing it now also prevents you from having to repeat the instructions to every single person as the day goes on.

Bend the arms at the elbow so the flowers sit slightly below waist level but on the side of the waist, not in front. Tell them it will feel weird but looks fantastic. Turn the body at a 45° angle so that the flowers are now pointed at the camera. This thins out the upper am and adds a separation from the body's core; which makes the waist look thinner.

For Men

Avoid the 'Fig-leaf' pose. You know what I'm talking about; that standing straight on with hands lowered and folded in front. This is not flattering, and makes it look like he has to use the restroom. Instead just do simple relaxed hands at the side.

If you want to break up the monotony of the basic black tux, try a few where the guy hikes a leg on a step, throw the jacket over the shoulder, or one hand in a pocket with the thumb sticking out (you don't want the whole hand in the pocket or it disappears completely.)

For Everyone

Stand tall, shoulders back, chins up – but not too far up.

Don't pose people straight on. This adds the appearance of weight. Pose them at a 45° angle, and then add the 'T' stance mentioned above.

If you are shooting a close-up of hands, try to avoid shooting a flat hand. Instead try to position the hand so that it is from the side and slightly curved.

If you do a close-up of faces there are 5 perfect face angles. *See examples included.

Straight on

Profile left

Profile right

¾ left (When it's correct, the side eye is on the outer edge and the nose doesn't cross over that line.)

¾ right

If you have a voluptuous person, a flattering sitting down pose would be to shoot down on him or her and have them look slightly up at you. This stretches out the throat area and immediately hides any double chins.

Likewise if you have an extremely thin person and want to add more substance, pose him or her more straight on that the 45° mentioned earlier. This will broaden the shoulders.

If you have extremely tall or short people paired together, ex: flower girl and groom, have the taller person sit down or kneel next to the smaller person.

When you are doing the gigantic extended family pictures right after the ceremony, one way to make things easier for yourself is to make a quick announcement and say, "Please pair up or group together with who you belong to (spouses, couples, families). This will make it easier for me to place you in the big group photo." Then you add small groups of people to the big group instead of spending time trying to place people individually.

Follow a basic formula of far-away, ¾ length, half-length, close-up for just about everything. This will give good variety and is easy to remember when things get hectic. (The only time I don't follow this is before the ceremony. Those I usually just do half-length and family pictures after the ceremony are full length.)

Do a last look for small details

- Fly away hair
- Wayward strings
- Bra straps
- Disappearing handkerchief squares
- Sideways flowers
- Sideways ties
- Power cords in the background
- ANYTHING odd in the background

Yes, you could Photoshop it later but it's easier to nip it now. Take two shots of everything in case someone has their eyes closed. Sometimes I'll do three but remember you're on a tight schedule so don't get carried away taking too long on each shot. If I've said this a thousand times, it's only because I want it to sink into your head. Weddings are a different beast. It's not your private studio time. You are not on a magazine shoot. Your subjects are not professional models. They are real people who are in a high stress environment, and are probably getting hungry and possibly cranky by now. You have to do your best to be professional, pleasant, and efficient. You have to be a comedian to get the real smiles, and you have to do it all at 90 mph with a good attitude. The better you become at getting a system down, the better off you'll be.

In the next section I have some image examples that might help visualize some of the posing angles.

VISUAL EXAMPLES

DO & DON'T POSING TIPS

Don't

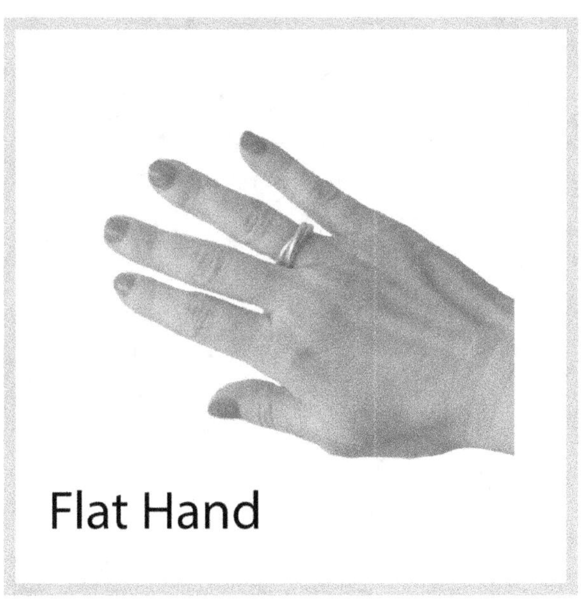

Example of a flat hand

Don't photograph hands like this unless you are wanting to add the appearance of extra weight.

Do

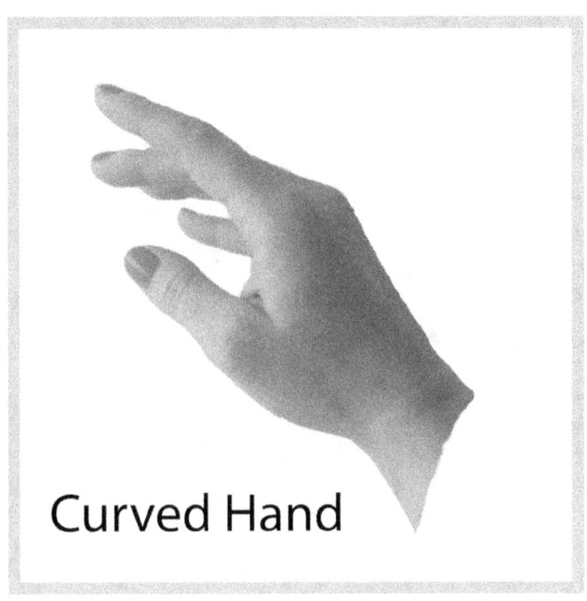

Example of a hand's side profile

Do photograph hands like this! The curved fingers and wrists are more flattering. This lengthens the fingers and adds dimension.

Don't

Example of someone standing with parallel straight forward feet

Don't have people stand like this for group pictures unless you are looking to add weight, stockiness and a straight body line.

Do

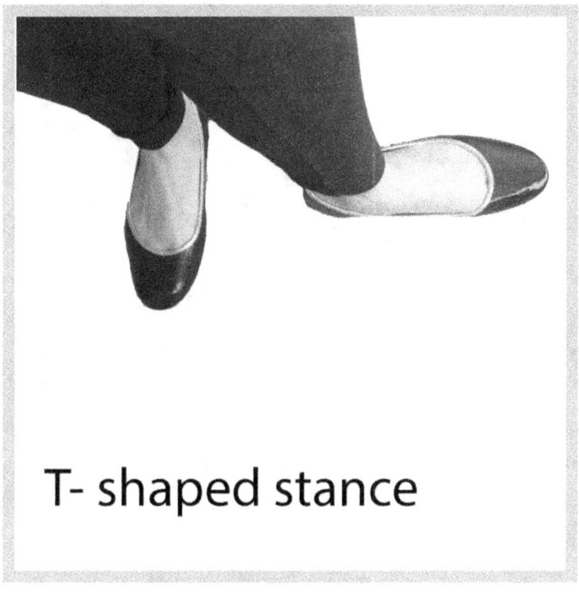

Example of someone standing with their back foot
perpendicular to their front foot

Do have them stand with their back foot sideways and their front foot pointing toward the camera. This works especially well if you want to create more 'curves' on the body line.

I usually get everyone standing in the right spot then announce, 'Ok Ladies who want to have thinner waists, put your feet in the shape of a 'T'. Put your weight on your back leg and let your front foot relax and point toward the camera. This is how you get that 'S' curve you see on super models."

VISUAL EXAMPLES

Do

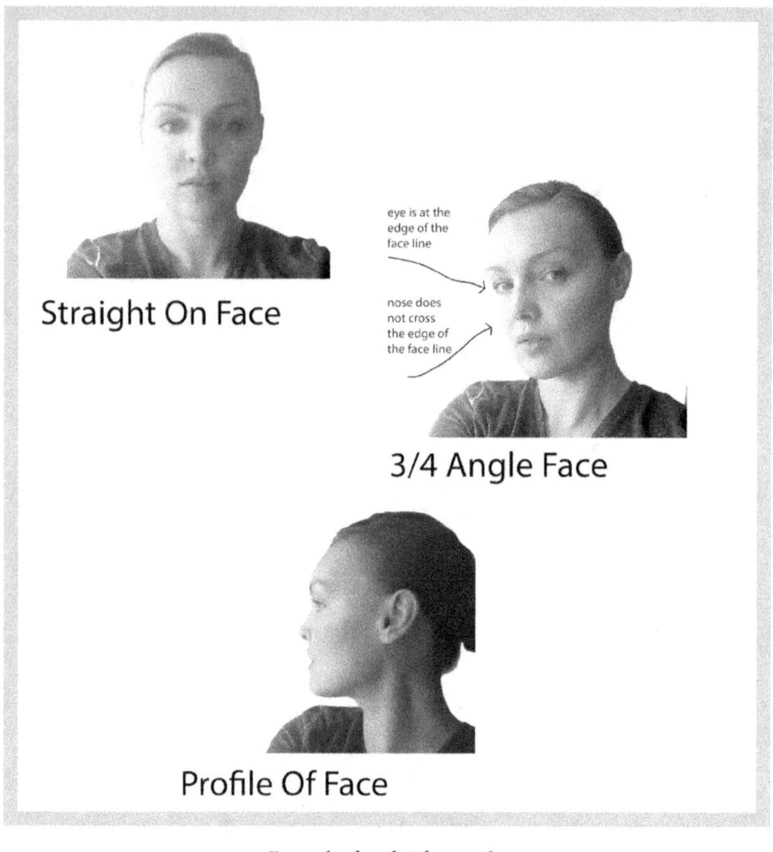

Example of perfect face angles

These are the 5 perfect face angles.

1. Straight on

2. Right 3/4 turn

3. Left 3/4 turn

4. Right profile

5. Left profile

14. FAMILY AND WEDDING PARTY INFORMATION

This form can be given to the clients, but should be filled out and returned ASAP. You will go over this again on the phone with the couple a few days before the wedding to make sure everything is still accurate.

Wait until a few days before the wedding to print it out because this information has been known to be changed at the last minute; this is especially true of people who are in the wedding party. Take the final form with you the day of and keep it in your clipboard. Use this to address people by name when you are gathering them for pictures. You don't have to memorize everyone's name, but at the very least, you should memorize the couple's names and their parent's names. To make people feel comfortable, start with their formal first name, then ask how does he or she prefer to be addressed. If all else fails and you forget the parent's names, it's OK to just call them Mom or Dad.

FAMILY AND WEDDING PARTY INFORMATION FORM

Download and edit your own at: https://drive.google.com/file/d/1v9jlFAyAE8qxN-zQ8-F9uiq77ct_w2gY/view?usp=sharing

This form can be taken home with the clients, but should be filled out ASAP. You may need to call the venues and make sure the addresses are current, etc.

Please complete and return ASAP

Bride:

Groom:

FAMILY

Bride's Parents:

Bride's Grandparents (Who will be present):

Groom's Grandparents (Who will be present):

Bride's Siblings (please put a check by those IN wedding):

WEDDING PARTY total #:

Maid of Honor:

Flower Girl:

Bridesmaids:

1:

2:

3:

4:

5:

Best Man:

Ring Bearer:

Groomsmen:

1:

2:

3:

4:

5:

Wedding Officiate:

Programs/Guest Book:

Additional VIP's:

:

:

Notes: (i.e. divorce, remarried, deceased, estranged, etc.)

:

:

:

:

(Ask questions about this section and get good details. You don't want to end up on someone's 'bad list', especially if they are the ones paying you. The last thing you want is to unknowingly pose people next to each other that can't stand to be next to each other. Taking the time to address this shows professionalism.)

15. AFTER IT'S ALL OVER

For you it means you get to work on post production. For the bride it could turn into Post Wedding Depression. Weddings are happy occasions. Before the event people are brimming with excitement for their big day. There's so much to do. And when things come together like puzzle pieces, it can be very gratifying. Then the event happens. Weddings are beautiful, sometimes extravagant, and always memorable. But then they are over in a flash. Every single bride says the same thing, "I can't believe it's over. It took me so long to plan it and now it's finished. The day just went by so fast!" Most, if not all, couples focus their attention on beginning the next chapter of their lives as newlyweds, but on rare occasions, there is a dark side - Post Wedding Depression sets in.

Keep your eyes open for signs of post wedding depression. It may not be a specific condition studied by research yet, but we in the biz have seen it happen with our own eyes. If you think this is hogwash, consider this. Some people have spent months, sometimes years, planning their wedding day. They've spent enormous time, effort and resources to make it perfect. Sometimes when it's all over they think they have nothing else to look forward to, or at least they don't think they do. Again, this is very rare, but something you would never know unless someone told you about it, or you experience it for yourself so it is worth mentioning.

In this state of post wedding depression some people will nit-pick and look for things to complain about with your service just to try and get some money back to ease the guilt of their recent overspending on the entirety of the event. You can't take the dress back, you can't return the songs played at the wedding, the flowers are dried out, the cake has been eaten. But photographers are one of the only wedding vendors that clients still work with after the ceremony.

By all means if they have a legitimate complaint, do your best to work with them until both parties are happy. If you messed up, it is in your best interest to do everything in your power to make them happy including giving a refund. Ask what specifically they dislike about the photographs or the service you provided. Was it a miscommunication? Can you fix it? Is it sincere, or is it something else? Since you should be encouraging an open line of communication with your clients, you shouldn't have this problem. But if you are hearing things after the wedding like, " Well we just don't like the way we look, we can't explain why, we just don't like the pictures, etc. We want a refund." These are signs that they might be having buyer's remorse or a deeper issue.

The key is to have an open line of communication so that you avoid these scenarios later and try to select good clients from the beginning. These are very rare cases, and most of the things people could complain about can be avoided with proper planning upfront so that they don't happen in the first place. It is when people feel they are let down or that you didn't hold up your end of the bargain that they complain, so wouldn't you want to do everything possible so that this doesn't happen? Of course you would!

That being said, we must also keep in mind the reality of wedding expenses and the lengths some people go through to have 'the perfect day.' Some people mortgage their homes for funds just for this event and when it's over they might have buyers remorse. This is sad, but it happens. And it's unfortunate for you because you are not a commodity, you are a service provider. It's not like you can take your day back and stock it back up on the shelf for the next buyer like you could a physical item such as a sofa.

You worked just as hard at that wedding as you did for the cute couple that was truly in love and had a glorious easy-to-photograph day. Finding the right fit before you sign any contracts will help you and you business for the long run.

However, sometimes you can plan for the best and the unthinkable happens. I once had a bride come in after the wedding to pick up everything and she got really angry and upset looking at the pictures. She pulled out all the stops and demanded a refund. I tried to assure her by telling her of course we want her to be happy and we will do whatever we can to fix it including giving a refund if necessary.

But she couldn't tell me what we did wrong. She remained very vague and couldn't pinpoint any specific issues. Things were getting heated. I told her I was going to leave the room to give her a few minutes to collect herself and then we can try again on finding a solution that would make her happy. I said if we did something wrong we will of course give you a refund, but you have to tell me what that 'wrong' was. She just kept saying I hate the pictures, I just want my money back.

I came back to the room a few minutes later and she was in tears. She apologized to me and said there's nothing wrong with the photographs, that we did a good job. She confessed that she and the groom had already split up and were living separately.

She couldn't bear to look at the photographs, but it had nothing to do with us. There's no tiptoeing around it. This situation stinks. As much as you might be tempted to give her money back out of pure sympathy, you have to remember that you did the job for which you were hired. You are running a real business and have financial obligations of your own.

Again, this is an extremely rare scenario but it really did happen; which means it could happen to you too. Knowing how to handle these delicate situations will prepare you for *if* they happen. More than likely it won't, and my hope is that you'll have perfect clients most of the time.

16. FINAL REMARKS

Congratulations! If you've read this far you are already more knowledgeable than when you started and that means something! You already know you won't become an expert overnight, but you also know you are taking the steps to become an expert with every wedding you photograph.

I know not all of this information will pertain to every wedding photographer out there, nor is this information meant to be the end-all-be-all guide, so go and find your niche! As I stated before, this is just how I've done it. If my knowledge through experience helps even one person, then it was worth writing it. I learned mostly through hands-on experience working for other professional studios. I took what worked for me and left behind what didn't. Now it's your turn to do the same.

Good Luck! When in doubt, just shoot like crazy and do your best to build good working relationships.

· · ·

I truly hope this guide helps you on your journey as a professional wedding photographer. There's more I could probably say on every topic, but some things you just have learn by doing and carve out your own way.

MISC. FORMS

Copyright Release

Download, edit and print your own at: https://drive.google.com/file/d/114ckiI8lSRGxePSyMRLOqG_DXw1eAflv/view?usp=sharing

Take this part out before printing. This is if you're client wants to put their wedding picture in a newspaper for an announcement. Not all papers will require it, but again, it's professional to offer it.

[Clients names]

Re: Copyright release

To whom it may concern:

This letter is to serve as a [one] time copyright release. [Your name or studio name] owns the

Copyright to the attached images described as:

and hereby agrees to grant permission for the images to be used for the purpose of producing as per selection of one or more of the principals in the photograph. The print or digital file cannot be used for any other purpose beyond the description above and this is a single use release. The appropriate representative from:

will abide by this release and any questions or concerns should be brought to the attention of [studio owner].

Thank You,

[Studio name]

[Your name]

[Address]

[Phone]

[Web]

[Email]

* * *

Model Release

Download, edit and print your own at: https://drive.google.com/file/d/12N1cFI2QOSQSQUKUVDa3t3_Mnm8aWKyB/view?usp=sharing

Take this part out before printing. You need this is you want to use their images as studio samples so it's better to get it now while you're signing the other paper work. You can also use this same release if you do other portrait work.

I, (insert the Model's name) do hereby give

(insert the Photographer's name), his or her assigns, licensees, successors in interest, legal representatives, and heirs the irrevocable right to use my name (or any fictional name), picture, portrait, or photograph in all forms and in all media and in all manners, without any restriction as to changes or alterations (including but not limited to composite or distorted representations or derivative works made in any medium) for advertising, trade, promotion, exhibition, or any other lawful purposes, and I waive any right to inspect or approve the photograph(s) or finished version(s) incorporating the photograph(s), including written copy that may be created and appear in connection therewith. I hereby release and agree to hold harmless the Photographer, his or her assigns, licensees, successors in interest, legal representatives and heirs from any liability by virtue of any blurring, distortion, alteration, optical illusion, or use in composite form whether intentional or otherwise, that may occur or be produced in the taking of the photographs, or in any processing tending toward the completion of the finished product, unless it can be shown that they and the publication thereof were maliciously caused, produced, and published solely for the purpose of subjecting me to conspicuous ridicule, scandal, reproach, scorn, and indignity. I agree that the Photographer owns the copyright in these photographs and I hereby waive any claims I may have based on any usage of the photographs or works derived therefrom, including but not limited to claims for either invasion of privacy or libel. I am of full age* and competent to sign this release. I agree that this release shall be binding on me, my legal representatives, heirs, and assigns. I have read this release and am fully familiar with its contents.

Client (sign):

Client (print):

Date:

Client (sign):

Client (print):

Date:

Photographer (sign):

Photographer (print):

Date:

Consent (if applicable)

I am the parent or guardian of the minor named above, and have the legal authority to execute the above release. I approve the foregoing and waive any rights in the premises.

Client (sign):

Client (print):

Date:

APPENDIX

Below are links to organizations or companies that have proven to be an invaluable resource for the career of the professional photographer. Some of the Associations may not be feasible for you at this point in your career, but that will be on a person-to-person basis. Before you join an organization, think of how much work you are currently getting as a professional. The monthly dues to these groups can be high, and if you can't afford that right now maybe wait until you get more work under your belt and a stream of regular clients. However if you can swing it, I would definitely recommend the Professional Photographers of America before any other group. I am an off and on member, depending on how much work I schedule out that year. This is the number one resource for us for many reasons.

Education – they are not a book and lecture school like a university. They offer the advice of real working professionals that deal with real world business situations.

The Network – All professionals belonging to this organization (in this area at least) are top notch. Like any job, the more 'better positioned' people you know, the better.

Equipment Insurance – Your homeowners insurance may not cover everything. PPA offers extensive equipment insurance specifically for our needs.

Indemnification – This might be one of the most important ones as it may save your business one day.

Professional Photographers of America

www.ppa.com

* * *

Equipment – Sales, Rentals and Repairs

If you're in the St Louis, MO area, I really like the folks at Schillers. They've been around forever, and you can rent equipment as well. This is my #1 retail source for equipment in St. Louis

Schillers

9420 Manchester Road

St. Louis, MO 63144

314-968-3650

http://www.schillers.com

B & H Photo

I used to go to their super store in NYC but you can get stuff Online as well.

http://www.bhphotovideo.com

Another good resource, especially on a tight budget is Ebay. You don't have to be a snobby 'gear head' about all the equipment you use. Some off brand stuff might be just fine for a while until you can afford to get the nice stuff. I've purchased off brand radio transmitter systems, light stands, filters, light meters, etc. for cheap and they've worked fine. It's also a good resource for used equipment. Ebay has buyer protection on some things, so you can get your money back if it's a dud. Consider a good used Nikon or Canon with lower mega-pixels for a back up camera.

www.ebay.com

* * *

Print & Presentation Services - Online Professional Print Lab, Sales, and Presentation Software that can be used on a per-job basis if needed. This is my number one resource if you are doing more than just giving your client a bundle of downloadable images. You can make a website with proofs for the client, they can order from the site, you can fulfill print orders, the prints can be mailed to you or directly to the client. It's a one-stop shop for everything 'post-production client related'.

https://power.n-vu.com/

WORKS CITED & WEBSITE LINKS

1. "Must-Take Wedding Photo Checklist." *Real Simple*, Real Simple Magazine, www.realsimple.com/weddings/ceremony/must-have-wedding-photos.

* * *

1. B & H Photo: http://www.bhphotovideo.com

2. Copyright Release: https://drive.google.com/file/d/114ckiI8lSRGxePSyMRLOqG_DXwieAflv/view?usp=sharing

3. Ebay: www.ebay.com

4. Family & Wedding Part Information: https://drive.google.com/file/d/1v9jlFAyAE8qxN-zQ8-F9uiq77ct_w2gY/view?usp=sharing

5. Model Release: https://drive.google.com/file/d/12NIcFI2QOSQSQUKUVDa3t3_Mnm8aWKyB/view?usp=sharing

6. N-Vu: https://power.n-vu.com/

7. Professional Photographers of America: www.ppa.com

8. Schillers: http://www.schillers.com

9. Sunset Calculator: http://www.timeanddate.com/worldclock/astronomy.html?n=605

10. Survey Maker Website: https://www.typeform.com/

11. The REAL Must Have Shot List: https://drive.google.com/file/d/18cg4gIBtpnWa5CZ3nWB-QljeCh74nfxF/view?usp=sharing

12. Wedding Contract: https://drive.google.com/file/d/1tXVs1zeXQvAquumWmGovHSGeHWX5Ms9c/view?usp=sharing

13. Website Maker Platform: www.wix.com

ABOUT THE AUTHOR

Reach out! Let me know if you found this guide helpful. How can I make it better? I'm on a few social media sites, albeit more active on some than others.

 twitter.com/rtistjen
 linkedin.com/in/jennifer-allison-a597a64a